Unspoken
WORDS
WILL
NEVER BE

Heard

JENNETTE SMITH

ISBN 979-8-88943-355-2 (paperback)
ISBN 979-8-88943-356-9 (digital)

Christian Faith Publishing
832 Park Avenue
Meadville, PA 16335
www.christianfaithpublishing.com

Printed in the United States of America

In loving memory of

Earlyne Gilmore
(April 06, 1957–December 18, 2019)

and

Gregory Gilmore
(December 30, 1980–December 1, 2019)

I love you forever.

Unspoken Words Will Never Be Heard was written during a dark time of my life—a time that I was broken, I was hurt to the point that my mouth could not utter the pain that I felt in my heart. A time that I didn't know if I was coming or going. I was just existing. My soul was restless, and I couldn't sustain it. I was unsure of what to do or who to turn to. Silently, I hid in the shadows of a fake smile that was being watered by rivers of tears daily. For a season, I felt lost. I felt lost because I was carrying a burden that was too heavy for me to carry, but it meant too much to me for me to let go. So I carried my burden day in and day out. Finally, I realized the weight was too heavy. I was suffocating, dying slowly when I desperately wanted to live. Unsure of who was for me or against me, I called on the only person that I felt I could trust. Even though I had let him down periodically, he still answered faithfully, and he still loved me unconditionally. I called on Jesus, and that day, I returned home to my Father, vowing to abide in him forever. The season that I had journeyed into was a place that I wanted no other woman to travel without being equipped for that season. I made it out by faith and by the grace of God. I was gracefully broken during my season so that I could discover my purpose and walk into my calling, which is to motivate other women who will eventually travel my journey, in hopes to encourage them not to give up and encourage them to endure what they are going through, because through that pain, a beautiful woman will emerge.

Proverbs 27:17 (NIV) proclaims, "As iron sharpens iron, so one person sharpens another."

I am here to encourage you and strengthen you in trials or areas of your life that you're struggling in. My prayer is that as you begin to read that your faith in God will be restored, and you will continue to fight until victory is yours.

1 Peter 3:9 (NIV)

Do not repay evil with evil or insult with insult.
On the contrary, repay evil with blessing, because
to this you were called so that you may inherit a
blessing.

Regardless of what you face in life, face it with a smile, never being defeated or discouraged by those who dug ditches in hoping you would fall, those who plotted against you in silence, not knowing that God heard them full blast, not knowing that what they meant for your harm backfired and God was using it for your good. The words that were meant to break you did the opposite and made you whole. Those who walked away from you made you realize that you could still survive without them. Instead of being distraught, you were content with being uprooted, because you knew who you were being deeply rooted in. Things you faced maybe didn't look good when you were trying to figure out how you were going to put the pieces of your life back together. You were uncomfortable when you were being detached and stretched, even though you hid your tears and pain from those who tossed you into the furnace, God used your ashes to strengthen you for your next season. You didn't realize it then, but because you withstood the mistreatment that you were receiving from others faithfully and because you continued to humble yourself once they turned up the heat in this season, God is going to use your enemies to bless you for everything you endured next season. Love your enemies even while trusting in God's promises.

Road Trip

Life is like taking a road trip. You thoroughly plan how you want things to go from your arrival to your departure. You pack according to the season and where you're going. You plan how you intend to get to your destination. You check if you will experience any layovers if you're traveling by plane or how many times you are going to stop to refuel and where, if you're traveling by automobile. You even plan for tourist attractions you want to explore. You have everything figured out and anticipate your big day, never planning for the unexpected. What happens in life when you have a three- to five- problem pileup? What happens when you must detour because one of those problems are taking longer to fix? What happens when your trip gets postponed because of a layover. What happens when you're forced to reschedule because a pandemic hits? Just like with a canceled trip, in life we get upset. We get bitter and angry because things are not going the way we intended. People we thought we would share life with walk away; jobs we thought we would retire at, we get fired from; death hits your family back-to-back; or for a season, your health declines unexpectedly. When we run into setbacks in life, we still need to continue praising God. We still need to continue praying. We still need to tell God, "Even though I don't know what you're doing or why you're doing it, I still trust you." Continue to have joy on your journey because those problems were just a test to see if your faith in God is unconditional. What you were planning was based on what you could afford. Where God is about to take you is based on what he can afford. Your layover was God preparing you for the rollover of blessings in your next season. On your road trips, expect delays and detours, trusting that despite of the unexpected, you will reach your destination in perfect timing.

Matthew 6:34 (NIV)

Therefore do not worry about tomorrow; for tomorrow will care for itself. Each day has enough trouble of its own.

A lot of times, we go through life living each day worrying about what tomorrow is going to bring or what the future will hold, when all God wants us to do is focus on today. When worrying, we make spur-of-the-moment decisions by assuming how things are going to turn out, but God already had the problem figured out before we faced the issue. We get in debt by making purchases that we don't need; we let go of people who were meant to be a part of our journey, but then we hold on to those who are hindering us. A lot of headaches and heartaches could be avoided if, instead of trying to figure things out or make plans based on our own understanding, we acknowledge God for who he is in our life. God is a present help in the time of trouble. The enemy wants you to live fearfully and doubt God, because if he can cause you to be nervous over little things, he knows that your faith is weak, and you won't let God direct your path into your calling toward bigger things. Stop worrying about tomorrow, and live your life today.

It's Not You, It's Him

We as women must start doing better with the men we choose to date, have kids with, or marry. We can no longer judge a man by how he treats himself, because under the mask, the good job, nice house, and fancy car stands a broken man who puts himself together the best way that he can in public. We can no longer go by how he treats his mom, because some men put on their best behavior around their mom. He's falsely representing himself around us. Others live their daily life with an invisible pacifier in their mouth and will always "need" his mom more than he "wants" you. Last but not least, some of their moms will know that they have a dark side, that she's responsible for creating, but it won't show its ugly face until you do something that reminds him of his mother. Then you will experience all of his misplaced hate, and you'll get abused though you were not the abuser. So, ladies, my advice to you is to find a man who believes in God and who is striving to be Christlike, because only then will he ever be able to love you the way that Christ loves the church. God gave us the ability to birth a child, not a full-grown man. We will never be able to create a perfect man, because we ourselves are not a perfect woman. A man must know God and strive to be who God ordained him to be before he was placed in the womb of his mother. A man must want to be a man and must have become a man before he ever met you, and you must be a real woman before looking for a real man.

Get Your Grove Back

How you feel and what you think about yourself affects how far you are willing to go to have a meaningful future. Sometimes we look at past mistakes or choices that we have made in life and allow it to hinders us. We allow it to offset the calling that God has on our life. Lack of feeling worthless will make you think that you deserve to be stuck in a season in which you bear no more fruit. It is planting your seed but receiving an insufficient harvest because you planted a seed of doubt, a seed of fear, a seed of shame—because you gave up on potential and possibilities. We use being married, a single mom, or growing up in poverty as an impediment and allow it to stop us from accomplishing our dreams. We let others tell us what we can't do, when Matthew 19:26 says, "With man this is impossible, but with God all things are possible." God will never call you to do something without equipping you with the knowledge and strength that you need to do it. Stop making excuses and feeling sorry for yourself, and be the woman that God created you to be. Be the woman that you know you can be. Get your grove back and make a difference in the world.

Galatians 6:9 (NASB1995)

Let us not lose heart in doing good, for in due
time we will reap if we do not grow weary.

I know that like me, you have bent over backward many times
to help other people, whether monetary, words of comfort, transportation, etc. Receiving not even a simple "Thank you" or "I appreciate
you in return." Despite of having barely enough to take care of your
own needs, you gave vigorously, because you didn't want to see them
unable to meet their need. You were amazed that once being put in
the same situation, those you did for and now needed were nowhere
to be found. You robbed Peter to pay Paul, as you spread yourself a
mile long and an inch deep, just to pull through your hard times.
Silently, they stood on the sideline, waiting for your demise. Despite
the mistreatment and because you have a kind heart, you continued
to help, you continued to allow yourself to be taken advantage of.
You sacrificed yourself as a burnt offering yet receiving no appreciating for going above and beyond or holding things down until their
situation changed. Sadly, you are disappointed that your name has
been slandered, considering you useless and have rendered no good
service to them. They are angry at you when you should be angry at
them, but instead you're angry at yourself. Even though a person's
actions have hurt you, continue to be you. Don't make any adjustments to the genuine person that God has created you to be. God
sits high and looks low. He saw you, and he's seen them, and he will
reward you both accordingly to your actions.

2 Corinthians 5:7 (NKJV)

For we walk by faith, not by sight

Oftentimes, we allow ourselves to get overwhelmed by things in life that we are facing. Some situations we see as being permanent, when they were only temporary. Once seeing no improvement, we get stressed over the downward spiral; and hastily, we try to fix things. But instead of making it better, truthfully, we only make things worse. We allow people to dictate how our story is going to end, and if it's something that we don't like, we began doing things out of fear, trying to get a different outcome. We get discouraged during the waiting phase of things working itself out. We pray faithfully, but because we continue to see the same situation, we stop praying, eventually giving up. We allow the voices of others to tell us we are wasting our time or what's not going to change. We fail not because what we were facing was God's will, but because we stop praying and believing not only in ourselves, but in God. We forget that situations change just like seasons change. We judge things on an outer appearance, never taking into consideration what God was doing behind the scenes. We get weary when God tells us not to worry. We give up when God said he has the final say. Stop looking at things by sight and start walking by faith, and those things will come to pass. Your season will not shift until you start facing your Goliaths and destroying them.

Revelation 2:23 (NIV)

I am He who searches the minds and hearts; and
I will give to each one of you according to your
deeds.

On your journey, you will be approached by a lot of people
whose only motive is to hinder you from reaching your destiny.
People will try to provoke you into quarrels that are irrelevant to
what God is intending to use to strengthen you. When those situations come, like an eagle you must rise above them. Misery loves
company, so don't get distracted by someone standing on the sideline. Stopping to entertain them will only steal your joy and cause
the rest of your day to go bad. Getting even will start to saturate your
mind, and eventually your mood will begin to change, because you
will have allowed that anger to fester in your heart and start taking it
out on people who didn't deserve it. Saying things you didn't mean,
finally reverting to the old you because you fell victim to Satan's tactics. That's why daily you must pray and ask God to help you to not
only recognize the attacks of the devil, but to also help you handle
situations in ways that are pleasing in his eyesight. There will always
be difficult people, some who will always get up on the wrong side
of the bed or some who only know being rude. But remember, you
can't control what they say, but you can control your response. Treat
people with kindness despite how they treat you. Allow God to be
your vindicator. Don't allow them to steal your joy over a temporary
altercation.

Ezekiel 37:46 (NIV)

Then he said to me, "Prophesy to these bones and say to them, 'O dry bones, hear the word of the Lord! This is what the Sovereign Lord says to these bones: I will make breath enter you, and you will come to life. I will attach tendons to you and make flesh come upon you and cover you with skin; I will put breath in you, and you will come to life. Then you will know that I am the Lord.'"

The season that you are in at this present time, you are experiencing it for a reason. You are facing it because of your previous actions. Despite everything that God has been doing for you, despite the situations that he brought you through and the countless times that he has spared your life, your faith in God has still been wavering. He has been trying to shift you into a new season, but you kept repeating the same cycles, you were still insisting that your way was better than his way. So now you're sitting in the dry season of your life, bearing no fruit. You see no rain clouds; all your worldly possessions have gone. You have been forsaken by friends and family, helplessly wandering. The foundation that you personally built has fallen like Babylon. The same way that you came into this world is now how you're left standing naked and alone. Like Lazarus, you have begun to smell. You're in a season that you have been declared dead. This time, when you make it out, you and everyone around you will know that it was only by the grace of God. When God brings you out this time, you will acknowledge him. You will allow him to direct your footsteps, leaning not on your understanding but trusting in him always. When God makes breath enter you and you come to life, you will know that he is Lord.

Romans 12:6 (NLT)

In his grace, God has given us different gifts for doing certain things well. So if God has given you the ability to prophesy, speak out with as much faith as God has given you.

Not realizing it, sometimes you will spend months or even years living in the shadows of someone else, pleasing them, but forgetting about yourself in the process. You have been trying to fit in when God's purpose for you was to stand out. You have dimmed your light to make others feel comfortable. Lowered your standards to uphold someone else. You decreased so they could increase, not knowing that God can't increase you any higher because you're doing nothing on the level you're at. God did not give you a gift to sit on the sidelines or to walk in the shadows of someone. You are allowing other people to make you feel insecure about who you are becoming, when your purpose could be to influence them. God created you for greatness, and he has placed a unique gift in everyone. Do what glorifies God and what makes your soul shine. Pray that through you, others will seek God for their self and discover their gift and hidden talents within.

Don't Break Down in Your Breakthrough

You might not believe what I'm about to tell you, because you have been battling one thing after another. Relief doesn't seem to be nowhere in sight and in your mind, you're wondering how much more can you take. How much longer can you pretend that you are okay, how much longer can you hold things together when your life is falling apart? Day in and day out, life reminds you that you are walking in the valley of the shadow of death. You're trying not to make eye contact with anyone because they will see a river of tears in your eyes that are ready to express what the heart feels but dares not mumble, so it sits in silence and breaks behind its chambers because nobody hears its cries for help. You no longer feel happy or sad—you're just angry. The days are changing, but time is standing still. Faithfully, you have been praying, interceding for others because they have not experienced God's greatness or accepted him in their life. You're praying for your situations continuously while waiting for joy to come in the morning. Your back is against the wall, yet your eyes are still to the heavens. You believe if you can just touch the hem of Jesus's garment, by your faith, circumstances would change. Regardless of how things look, hold on and keep pressing toward the mark. The same energy that you would use to go backward is all it takes to push forward. God is with you, and you will make it if you don't lose your faith and break down in your breakthrough.

Conquering Your Obstacle

I know that you have been facing obstacle after obstacle. Different day but the same season. The time is now for you to disconnect your feelings from your actions and trust in God. It is important that you realize that every adversity that you have been facing isn't meant to destroy you or for you to fight. Some are meant for you to approach differently and show others the difference that Christ has made in your life. Some are meant for you to stand back and humbly observe, because what's out to hurt you will eventually hurt themselves. A lot of times, in life, you keep facing obstacles because the enemy has paid attention to how you handle yourself every time an altercation or situation occurs. Once the water gets rough and the wind starts to blow, you retreat when there were only dark clouds in the sky but no rain, smoke but no fire. Some obstacles you gave up on approaching because you have allowed the size to intimidate you instead of remembering the God who has went before you and is willing to still go with you now if you show up willing to try. Some obstacles are small, but you have gotten discourage, because you are still carrying around the memories of defeat from a pass battle, so you surrendered upon arrival. Every obstacle that you face is an opportunity to improve your condition and secure your future. Obstacles are to strengthen you and increase your faith in God and your faith in yourself. Rather you go through your obstacle, over your obstacle, around your obstacle or under your obstacle. Get past your obstacle so your season can shift, and you can receive and live the life that God promised you.

No Matter What Happens, Keep Pursuing

Whenever you are trying to get yourself and your life together, the enemy will come to attack. The enemy will try to sabotage everything that you are trying to accomplish. The enemy will send people in packs, to attack you from all sides, blocking your view so you can't see your way out. His main intention is blocking the light, he's trying to convince you that you are in a cave, instead of a tunnel. The enemy's purpose is to kill, steal, and destroy. You are on a mission and no matter what happens keep moving because delay does not mean denied in God's sight. Rely on the promises that God made to you, remember that God is our refuge and strength, a very present help in trouble. With confidence draw near to the throne of grace for help. In your time of trouble encourage yourself, speak life into your situation. No matter how things look, continue to believe that everything is going to be alright. Keep pursuing because better days are coming. God is Alpha and Omega, and nobody can stop what God has put in motion. Your best weapon against the enemy is prayer.

Greatness Attached to Transition

You will feel overwhelmed when going from comfort to calling. You're comfortable because you don't want to change your surroundings. You don't want to find new friends; you don't want to start over at a new job. You don't want to let go of a toxic relationship. You have got comfortable with being comfortable. If God did not push you, you would never alleviate to your next level. You would never accept your calling because you're comfortable. The reason shifting into your calling is harder than you expected is because you're wasting more time trying to do things your way instead of the path that God created for you. You're trying to take people into a season that you are meant to be alone in. You feel stretched because you are being pulled by your past but called by your future. Stop allowing distractions to interfere into a season that God got you covered in. Stick with the plan that God has for you. Your blessing will always be in where you are going, not where you started. Let go of your past and move into the greatness that's attached to your transition.

Reverse Your Speech and God Will Reverse Your Curse

Before knowing better, before the transforming and renewing of your mind. You spoke some things over your life that you didn't know were connected to your destiny. You spoke some things over your marriage, over your relationships, over your kids, over your finances, over your health, and over your family. Now you are sitting in situations with no clue on how to get out. You are wondering why everything is off balance in your life. Instead of prospering, things are quickly deteriorating. You are praying, but the things you are praying for you see no change in. You are waiting for better days, but instead things are only getting worse. The reason things are not progressing is because you spoke death in the areas that you should have spoken life. You poisoned the vision and destroyed the dream. You have damaged the crop that you were in charge of planting, with the deadly chemicals that came out of your mouth. Your words have power and for things to get better you need to repent, you need to ask God to forgive you and start speaking life over your situation, start back believing, start encouraging and lifting those that you have put down. Those who dream that you have crushed help them put the pieces back together. It may take time to undo what you have done, but don't give up. God hears your prayers. He sees your tears, and he knows your heart. Continue to reverse your speech, and God will reverse your curse. Things will get better in due time.

John 15:16 (NKJV)

You did not choose me, but I chose you.

We should feel privileged that God believed in us enough to have chosen us for such a time like this. He entrusted us with being a positive influence on those who do not believe, knowing that his light would shine bright and radiant through us using the unique gift that he has given us. God knew that our trials would lead to our testimony and our testimony would lead to our breakthrough. We would excel when others thought we would fail, we would live when others thought that we would die. God believed in us even during the times we didn't believe in ourselves. Even though our journey wasn't perfect, God loved us enough to direct our footsteps and got us back on track while strengthening us in all the areas that we were weak in. I pray that you feel just as special as I do with knowing that despite how we used to be that, God found us worthy enough to clean us up and use us for his glory. There is still a lot for us to learn and a lot of souls for us to draw. We will always be a target, and the enemy will never give up. Adversities will come, but they too shall pass. If you stand firm and your foundation is solid, he will always be defeated. Stay focused and stay encouraged, because what you are facing is something God already knew that you would be victorious in. That's why God chose you.

Stand Firm

Your future is determined on how you make it out of this season. If you are going through adversities at this moment in your life and you just can't seem to catch a break, I need for you to increase your prayer life and get into the Bible, because knowledge is power. The best way to fight what you're up against is to fight it with the word of God. Don't just read it allow the words to simmer into your mind, simmer into your soul, and store it in your heart. No matter what you're going through there is only two options, either it breaks you or you break it. The trouble that you're going through is because God got a calling on your life and that has now made you wanted. And if you're going to be wanted by the enemy, then be considered armed and dangerous. Let the enemy know that you're not going down without a fight. Prepare yourself with the armor of God, refusing to judge your situation by sight. Right now, it feels like it's you against the world, rest assured because during it all you are not alone, there are other prayer warriors and angels camped out. What you are going through, you have already walked through prior—different day but the same devil. It's the same devil because you have been giving up during the battle, giving up because you didn't know the battle has already been won, you just needed to believe that you could make it through it. You needed to realize that God would not take you through something that he wasn't going to bring you out of. That's why I am encouraging you now to stand still and know that God has everything under his control. The people who leave during your battle was never with you. The things you lose have no true value. Things may look big, but it is not bigger than the God we serve. Don't allow anything to distract you in your battle, because that is what the enemy wants. Before my breakthrough, I had to pray numerous times throughout my day and repeat scriptures to myself reminding myself that this too shall pass.

Even If You Don't Receive, Rejoice

We take a lot of things to God in prayer and stand with expectation that he will bless in our favor. Sometimes we are interceding on other's behalf in hoping that God will bless them, heal them, or save them, because we have been watching the downward spiral of their life. Then there are other times that we are asking him to shift things around in our life—rather, it consists of giving or taking. You must realize that there are somethings in our life that God will not shift because it is meant to shape us into who he created us to be. It's meant to grow us in areas of our life that we are weak or have allowed ourselves to get comfortable in. We need to step back and look at some of the things that we ask God to give us and then look around our neighborhood or poverty-stricken areas, focusing on those who are less fortunate and don't have. Yet out of greed, we are asking for more or putting specifics on our wants instead of appreciating what we have. Things that we need, we should evaluate those as well and think of what we are doing to achieve it ourselves, are we going after it or are we sitting still feeling entitled waiting of God to give it to us. Faith without work is dead. Rather we receive the things that we ask God for or not, we should be grateful that he gave us the gift of life. If we obey God and live a righteous life, God will bless us abundantly in due time.

The Process of Elimination

God's purpose and calling over your life is something that you have no control over. You will experience things that you do not understand and sit in seasons that seem like a lifetime. Part of you will feel as if you got this, while another part of you feels an emotion that is unexplainable as you try to get comfortable with the shift. It's a hard pill to swallow once you get a glimpse of the people who stabbed you in your back. Once you hear the voice of those who express how much they hate your very existence. You feel alone, until you finally accept the realization that you have been alone, even when you weren't alone. You had only been drawing everlasting strength from the word of God. Once you realize that without God, you would have never made it, you then began to thank him for never forsaking or leaving you. You thank him because even though others have hurt you by expressing how they don't need you. You're grateful and find joy in knowing that God needs you and his purpose for you and your life is far greater than what you could have ever imagined and you will be blessed with more than you have ever lost. Concentrate on what God says, and that will eliminate everything and everyone else that tries to destroy and discourage you from being great.

Bad Apples

There are times that God will step in our life and sort out the good apples from the bad ones, removing those that are damaged because if not, the entire batch will go bad. We don't know a person's heart or intention, but because of our heart, we will stay connected to people and things that are damaging us, things that are hurting us more than the naked eye can see. We try to help people because of love. We try to pull out the greatness that is in them, not realizing that a person has to want to save themselves. A person has to want better and do better at achieving those things. A person has to want it for themselves—if not, you will spend your entire life being their life support, resuscitating them every time they lose the urge to survive and just want to give up. God has better things for us, but as long as we refuse to let go of what or who we don't need, God can't give us better. So he will intervene and remove the bad apples that will spoil the entire batch, that are hindering you from what God called you to do. We have to realize that when we pray about situations in our life that God will either remove it or fix it. If he removes it we have to trust his process, if he's going to fix it we have to stand still and trust in God's timing, remembering that everything works together for our good and that he makes no mistakes. In its season, good apples will grow again. Until then, be thankful that God removed the bad ones.

Dead Weight

There comes a time in life that you will have to walk away from people. Rather it's friends, family, or a toxic relationship, eventually you will have to make a decision to say "I'm done." Especially when the burdens you are carrying are the weight of someone else's heartaches, hurt, and pain of someone else's trauma. You have to make the decision to walk away, not because you don't love them, but because God saw the path that you were headed down and opened your eyes so you could see you. God reminded you who he created you to be before placing you in your mother's womb. In the process not only did you realize your worth, but you got your self-esteem back and rediscovered that the love you have for yourself was worth more than the energy you have been wasting fighting trying to love someone with a hardened heart. Faithfully you have been trying to convince them to see that it's not too late to change. You have endured so much emotional abuse and verbal abuse until finally you realize the torture is no longer worth it. You accept the fact that loving them will always be impossible if they don't love themselves. Finally, you broke the chains in your heart that once held you bound and let go of the dead weight. The new you began to emerge from what once held you captive.

Accept It for What It Is

Everybody is not qualified to go where God plans on taking you, so until you start to clear out your circle, God can't bless you the way that he wants to. God can't open up the floodgates of heaven for you because you have so many people in your circle until you'll miss your blessing. You'll miss your blessing because you're not focused on the promises God made to you or the dreams he placed in your heart. You're concerned about other people being great. You're focused on them when they care less about you. You have been making yourself a doormat. Not only are people walking over you, but you have become a personal dumping ground for excess garbage. It is time for you to start concentrating on yourself. Concentrate on the things that God has promised you. Concentrate on the doors that God will open if you faithfully obey him. Life is too short. It is time for you to stand on your own. Time for you to want more. Time for you to unlock every door that God has placed in front of you. Everybody is not for you. Accept it for what it is and move on, instead of being a people pleaser, doing things that make them feel good. Learn how to serve, and that is doing things that make you feel good by doing.

The Silent Season of Testing

We all will experience a season that we will go through, and instead of there being chatter, you will only experience silence. A season of praying, but seeing no change in your circumstances. A season of talking to God, but it seems like you are getting no response. A season of trying to fix a part of your life that is broken but receiving no effort, so you feel alone. You feel weary because instead of words of encouragement, you're only being told by the opposition that what you're standing in need of is not going to happen and you're wasting your time hoping. You're trying to be strong, yet your heart feels as if you're slowly dying. You're watching the sunrise in everyone else's life while your skies are still dark. You can't move into your tomorrow because you haven't figured out how to get through your today. So you sit in your silent season silent because you don't know what else to do. In your silent season you must remember that even though you feel alone that you are not alone. God is waiting for the right time to bring you back to life. The right season to show you that his best work in your life was being done in silence, once God starts to bless you, you're going to move in silence, you're not going to have to explain how you made it or what God done for you, because his glory will shine through you. The silent season is hard, but don't rush it to pass. In due time, it will pass, and everything you lost will be replaced.

Beautiful Ashes

You may feel as if you have been in the furnace for a long time, burning off the parts of you that has been hindering you from walking into your calling. Burning off all the negative words that has been spoken over you throughout your life. Burning off old hurt, old mindsets, old friends, old behaviors. Burning off everything that wasn't Christlike in you so that you can influence others by allowing them to see that greater is he who is in me. Even though you have been in the furnace, Jesus has been in there with you. Restoring you, building up your confidence, creating boldness in you, a more creative version of you, a stronger you, a better you. You might not like the furnace, but you are being renewed so that God can use you for his purpose when you come out the furnace. You want look like what you been through only beautiful ashes will be the remembrance of the price you paid.

Pass Hurt

When things hurt us, we must make sure that we heal the correct way, stop saying "I'm okay," knowing truthfully you are not. Pretending you're happy, when deep down you are angry. You are angry because you went against your mind and your heart allowed itself to be vulnerable only to be let down. We must make sure that we search our hearts and release the hurt, release the residue of bitterness that other people have caused you when you allowed your heart to love. Release the pain that you experienced during childhood from a parent or relative, and allow yourself to outgrow your hurt. Yes, we pretend to be strong, because that helps us cover up the damage that was caused, but if we don't allow God to step in and search us completely, leftover pain will fester in our hearts for years, attacking every person that it comes in contact with. It will have others paying the deadly price for a crime they didn't commit. We don't realize how much extra baggage we carry around daily. Carrying it for support on a journey it's not needed on. We keep it hidden until the wrong button is pushed or wrong word have been mumbled and we attack. We release the pressure of all the misplaced anger, but we released it on someone who only purpose was to love you. A person that God sent, but you pushed away because you were overloaded with baggage from your past. Go to God in prayer and cast your burdens upon him so he may soften your heart and allow you to trust again. Love is a beautiful thing when shared with the right person, but you will never experience it until you let go of pass hurt.

Get on My Level

Regardless of who is cheering you on, always be your number one fan. You cannot depend on other people to show gratitude or be happy for your achievements in life. You can't expect people to support you or always believe in your dreams or talents. Your gifts are unique. They are precious gifts that God placed in you for you alone to excel. Despite what others have or where they may be at in life, never envy or compare yourself to them because who you are is more than enough. Be happy with the wonderful person that God created in his image. You may have some unexpected things that occur in your life, but never get discouraged, never question God or not appreciate the many blessings he has already given you, because greater is coming if you remain faithful and trust in God to direct your path. Never allow anyone to make you feel guilty or doubt the beautiful woman that you are becoming. Run your own race, and you will always be victorious at doing it. Always strive for greatness never settling at being comfortable because you were fearfully and wonderfully made. You will experience people who will be intimidated by the light that shine in you, intimidated that even in chaos you still manage to find joy. Even when being knocked down, you continue to get up with grace. Never dim your light for anyone, make others get on your level instead of bowing down to theirs.

The Becoming

In pursuit of becoming who you were created to be, you will find that many will not be able to journey with you. It is a journey that consist of you putting God first and then yourself. It's a journey that, instead of pleasing and making sure that others are happy, that you will have to become bold, confident, and courageous. You will have to make sure that you're happy, make sure that your wants and needs are a priority and no longer an option. You have probably been living life only being comfortable with being content, because you have been trying to help others expand to their full potential, while neglecting yourself. For years many people have loved the ideal of being in control of you. Knowing that no matter what or how they treated you, that you would always be there, allowing yourself to be their personal dumping ground. God saw that you were devaluing yourself and allowing yourself to be taken advantage of and that is why you have been walking in the season you were in, because God needed you to realize your worth. God needed you to realize that you deserve better, but most of all, God wanted you to want better. In your season, God has given you a purpose. You have grown into an amazing woman, and God wants you to inspire other women. He wants you to help them realize that they too are beautiful. Help them be the best woman that they can be in a world that will always find a reason to discredit them. Inner growth is something that can only be achieved and never removed after becoming.

Good Seeds

We continue to pray for things that are already ours, but we won't receive these until we stand in expectation. God has a lot of blessings stored up, waiting to give those to us for the seeds we planted while standing in a dry season. For the seeds we planted when we didn't see any changes, but we kept believing. For the seeds we planted when we were being overlooked, but we kept pursuing. For the seeds we planted despite how we were treated. God rewards us when we obey him, but one of the things we do not realize is when things take too long to come to pass, we allow our faith to wander and in the process our actions start to show that we don't believe in what we asked God to do is going to happen, so we start making other arrangements. We start talking negative as if we didn't want the blessing anyway. We start second-guessing the promises that God made us. We allow doubt to creep in where faith once lived. We must be able to realize when the enemy is planning a secret attack and rebuke him the minute discouragement comes across our mind. God tells us that we will harvest plentiful from the seeds we sow, but he doesn't tell us when to expect it. Waiting is our testing time, and being faithful in the waiting is our task. Continue planting good seeds despite your trials because even though you can't see it, rain clouds are forming, and God will bless you for every good seed you have sown in due time.

Repaid for All

Never think that God hasn't been paying attention to all that you have endured in this season of your life. God saw who all mistreated you and left you in your darkest hour, when they held the key to your light. God saw those that pretended that your best interest was at heart, while secretly stabbing you in your back. God saw the overflow of tears before they ever left your eyes. He saw the heartaches and headaches that ran rampant in your thoughts. God saw the lonely nights that you spent, faithfully praying and waiting on your season to shift. Losing weight not because you were dieting, but stress was eating you alive. He saw you continuously motivating yourself because nobody knew the difference that an ounce of encouragement would make. God saw you getting back up each time that words knocked you down. He saw you severely bruised but not broken. He saw you misguided but not lost. God saw your hopes and your dreams as you laid them aside, just to give something else time to grow. You may be looking over your life and feeling that you have nothing to show for all the things you invested in, but God wants you to know that nothing you have lost was in vain, he will repay you for everything that the locust destroyed in due time, and when you reap your harvest, it won't be partial. God is going to repay you for all.

Your Prayer Life

Even though we are supposed to pray daily, a lot of times, we take things for granted; we rush throughout our daily life forgetting to pray. Forgetting to keep our lines of communication open with God. We constantly tell ourselves that we will start back tomorrow, feeling that we got all the time in the world, until we are faced with a season that we were expecting to shift out of winter, but then unexpectedly winter repeats itself. We are faced with a hard freeze that our prayer life wasn't prepared for. Adversity after adversity overtakes us. Now we're standing battling a season that we are not equipped for, cold, afraid, and alone. We are trying to reopen our relationship with God while feeling ashamed because we knowingly put him off. Now were hoping that our selfish actions don't affect his response in him hearing and answering our prayers. God tells us that like a roaring lion, the enemy is always lurking, out to kill, steal, and destroy, with that knowledge our prayer life needs to always be on point. We need to pray throughout our day. Asking God to protect us from the seen and the unseen. Don't allow the enemy to catch you off guard and stuck in a season that you should be standing bold and firm in, with expectancy of your situation to shift, but instead you're standing there with a mustard seed of faith. Holding a weapon, but with no ammunition. Prepare yourself for the good days and the bad days, leaving no stone unturned. Don't go through life thinking that you can handle your own affairs and return to God as needed. Allow God to lead you, so you would only face things that's needed on your journey instead of things and problems you created by walking out of God's alignment. Stay in constant prayer with the God who can do all things but fail.

God's Will

Regardless of what you face in life, you must face it with confidence and grace, knowing that rather God give or take something away that you felt you needed to survive, you must humbly be satisfied with his decision. Even though we make plans and think that we know what the future holds or what's best for us, at the end of the day we don't know. God has already planned our life from start to finish. Anything that we go through he already knows the outcome of. He knows our heart and our thoughts before we ever show any type of expression. That's why he tells us to seek him and lean not on our own understanding but to acknowledge that he is God and to trust him to direct our steps. A lot of difficulties we face in life, we bring them on ourselves. We act out of frustration, greed, and being impatient. We compete and run races that weren't ours to run, when God only wanted us to be still. We involve ourselves in other people's lives and allow their problems to become our problems. We allow them to bring us down by concerning ourselves with what they think about us, when God tells us that if we stay with him, we are safe. We must always obey God and gracefully accept the things he does for us and give us because we know that we don't deserve it and we know that there are other people that are less fortunate. Rather we agree or don't agree just know that whatever is happening in our life it must happen for us to reach our destination. Quit changing God's plan expecting a better outcome and accept his will for your life.

Continue Standing

Sometimes when going through things in life, you will look around and notice that you are the only one still physically standing. The only one still fighting and waiting on a situation to come to pass. You're the only one still believing in the small glimpse of hope that God showed you in a dream that your season was going to eventually shift. Despite how it looks and despite how it's starting to smell, continue standing. It's easy for others to sit and tell you what to do or how you should handle a situation, because it's not them whose heart is in turmoil. They don't have anything to lose. They don't have anything invested. The trials teach us a lot—most of all, it shows us where a person's loyalty lies, it shows us who truly has our back when things get rough, and it shows us who to cut off once things get better. Problems in life will destroy your foundation if you are not anchored in God. Mentally and emotionally, it will break you down to your core. When the heart and mind is involved you will have to fight the battle spiritually, because if not, the enemy will allow depression to set in and wipe out your very existence. Once you overcome your situation, never allow yourself to be put in that position ever again. Only trust in God because he was your refuge and your strength in your time of need and it is because of his grace that you're able to tell how you made it through. Don't give in, continue standing. Soon it will come to pass.

Tuning Out the Chatter

Even though you can't shut the world off, there are times that you will have to tune everyone around you out. Just to take out the background noise so that you can stay focused and give birth to the gift that God put in your heart. A lot of the time our family and friends sit in content, enjoying everyday life until you have a dream that you want to pursue. They will cheer you on faithfully until it's time for that dream to take root. That will be the moment that the negative chatter will start. You will then be able to see that not only do you have to watch the company that you keep, but you will also have to quiet the voices that are around you. You will notice that blood is not always thicker than water, and it will become even harder to tell your friends from your enemies. Due to some people being envious, you can't listen to the outside chatter because the chatter is trying to convince you that you will never make it, the chatter will tell you that you're wasting your time, the chatter will tell you that nobody is going to support you. In hoping that you will give up and abort your mission. If God put a dream in you, he placed it in you for a reason and despite how anybody feels about you, they can't stop you from accomplishing that dream unless you fail to try and unless you refuse to believe. Don't allow the naysayers to cause you to doubt the promises God made you. Don't get discouraged, just tune out the chatter.

Trials in the Testing

You cannot go through life expecting everything to be given to you, blessings with no battles, gifts with no gratitude, or trails with no testing. You must realize that anything you acquire easily has no real value. So when you go to God in prayer and expecting an extraordinary blessing, expect for there to be some trials that you will face in the testing. Expect that when walking in your calling that it will cost you, your choice on receiving it turns into you having to decide how bad do you want it. God likes to know that we will worship him despite our trials. If you will still be faithful in a season that you will spend walking through the darkest valley. Are you willing to sacrifice your house by selling it, knowing that having shelter your fate will lie in someone else hand. Will you still love him after you lose your mother and brother seventeen days apart. God wants to know if you would still trust in him to restore your marriage after letting it lay dormant for two years. Will you still praise him once he shifts around your friends, and you have none. Will you still want what God has for you once you see the trials that you will face in the testing. Remember what you're facing is temporary the blessings are worth the trials and the trials are only a test. Just thank God for bringing you through.

Pillow Talk

You will face moments in your life and have conversations that only God knows about and understands. Conversations that without you opening your mouth, God already knows the pain in your heart and the reason for each tear. You talk to God because you know that nobody can comfort you or love you like he does and like your souls is in need of. Spending countless moments in prayer, blocking out the vision of your surroundings as your mind tries to comprehend and digest that despite how things look, faith says you are going to make it out of your season alive and well. It's nice to have people that you can vent to, but when you're trapped in-between seasons it's honestly a waste of time discussing a situation, that they have no control over. Taking their advice, in a life that is not theirs to live. During a season that will be their spring, but your winter. How can they tell you how to handle each day, when hypothetically they don't know if either of us will be here tomorrow. So in your quiet time, talk to God. In your lonely time, talk to God. In your weary time, talk to God. In your darkest hour, you talk to God, because he is the only one that can tell you, "Fear not for I know the plans I have for you, plans to prosper you and not harm you, plans to give you hope and a future." God is the only one that can tell you that before he formed you and placed you in your mother's womb, he knew you. He is the only one that knows your today and your tomorrow, and that knows when he's going to bring you through this season of your life, so rest in his arms while he directs your footsteps. It might feel uncomfortable, but trust in God. We must learn to lean on God first, not just for some things, but for all things. The more faith we put in him, the sooner he will bring us out and allow our season to shift. Have pillow talks with God. He has a purpose for every conversation. Not only does he listen, but God cares.

Words Hurt

Regardless of how much you love a person, there will eventually become a time that you have to stand your ground and speak up for yourself. A time that you can no longer bite your tongue, especially when they have never spared your feelings or even acknowledge them despite what you have faced. Some people use their words not only to devalue you, but in hopes to destroy your self-worth in hopes to break you mentally so you could feel lower than they themselves already feel. Some people hate you, not because you are who they said you are but because you are who they want to be. Some people have been damaged to the point in early childhood until hurting others is all they know and being someone else is better than being their empty self. Those they come in contact with put up with their behavior only so they would not have to experience their rage. They walk around with no remorse, only an infatuated sense of being envied by others. They feel entitles, and they will flaunt their ego as if your existence is worthless. Once a person makes you feel that way, sometimes you have to make them accept their flaws and recognize the speck in their eye, and that will calm their rage and cause them to retreat. Continue to pray for those who are lost, because prayer changes people and situations.

Distractions

You are so close to your breakthrough, but adversities seem to keep coming. Trying to steal your joy. Trying to take your eyes off the prize. Trying to tell you that you are wasting your time. Trying to get you off track not because failure is in your future, but because greatness is in God's plans. The enemy will use whatever it needs to use, in hopes to stop you from reaching your destination. That is why the enemy sends distractions to exhaust you physically, mentally, financially, and spiritually. You have to make sure that your prayer life is just as strong as the foundation that you're standing on. Believe in yourself and that you can do all things through Christ who strengthens you. Get rooted into a good church. You don't have to find a huge church, find one that makes you feel like you're at home, get into your Bible and apply each scripture to your everyday life. Ask God to guide your footsteps then prepare yourself for the journey that God is about to take you on.

Stand in Authority

Even though it's said to treat others how you wish to be treated, that will always be easier said than done. No matter how nice you are or how much you avoid trying not to disrespect others or their feelings, some people are going to still be mean and rude to you. Some people are going to always try to cut you deep with their words having no remorse once the words leave their mouth. Hoping to intimidate you and that not only do you give up on the promises that God made to you, but to see if they could get you to default back into the old you. The old confrontational, "I'm not going to take your foolishness, and I'm about to cuss you out," old you. Before you do, analyze the situation and realize that you don't have to lower your standards or act out of character just to speak your peace. You don't have to let a person get away with putting you down, just so they can feel better about themselves. Only come in agreement with whom God said you are and believe in the promises that God made to you. Be bold and courageous, for the Holy Spirit will come to you.

It Ain't Over

I know that you might be feeling discouraged and feeling as if there is no way out of the situation that you're going through. You have been going through it for days, that turned into months, and eventually those months turned into years. Those are days of your life that you will never get back. It seems as if it has been one thing after another. Finances, job, health, kids…even the one you love has seemed as if they have left you for dead, left you tackling things that you were supposed to be facing together. People have turned their backs as if you have never known each other. Those who are left, are still trying to convince you what to do, when a lot of things are easier said than done, when it's not their situation. You have been spending the majority of your time talking to God, sometimes he responds; other times, he just listens. Either way, you enjoy his company because through it all, he has been there, He has been watching your every action, he has been counting your tear drops, those sleepless nights he has been rubbing your back, just so you would surrender to sleep. Most of all, God has been encouraging you to hold on, encouraging you that everything is going to be alright, he has been reassuring you that it ain't over because he has the final say. God has been sustaining you for a purpose greater than you can imagine, so what you're going through is only temporary. Continue to believe that better days are coming. No matter what you are going through, speak life into it and tell yourself that it "ain't over!"

A Storm Is Brewing

Anytime that God is getting ready to elevate you to another level or you have strengthened your faith and connection with God, be prepared because adversities will come out of nowhere. Like a storm surge, the enemy will push everything on you and as it leaves, suck everything out of you, hoping to drain you, spiritually, mentally, emotionally and physically. The enemy goal is to destroy you and he will use everything possible to discourage you, in hopes that you will decide that the journey you are about to make is not worth the trip. Not worth the agony, not worth the heartache, not worth the pain, in hoping you would decide it's too expensive and not worth the price to be paid. Before you make a permanent decision in a temporary situation. Realize that if that journey wasn't important, if that journey wasn't worth making, and if God wasn't going to bless you abundantly on that journey, then why is the enemy wasting all his energy on you? Instead of getting weary, put on the full armor of God and fight your storms head-on, because despite the torrential rain, the rough seas, or strong winds, always remember that Jesus is sleeping in the bottom of the boat.

Love is patient, love is kind. It does not envy, it does not boast, it is not proud. It does not dishonor others, it is not self-seeking, it is not easily angered, it keeps no records of wrongs. (1 Corinthians 13:4 NIV)

We as women must always remember our worth. Even though we don't want to be alone, we need to realize that being alone is far better than being in love with the wrong person. We can't brag about or be happy, being with somebody that doesn't value our worth. Someone that abuses us verbally with their words and emotionally with their neglect. Someone who cares more about putting us down, instead of picking us up. We pretend to be weak only to make them feel strong. We give them our all and we accept receiving nothing in return. Yet we love them, even though we are diming our light, just so they could shine. We need to realize that a real man would not need us to lower our value, as a power couple we will increase our worth together. We need to set examples for our daughters and sisters so that they will be young princesses and queens until they find a king who will carry some of the women's weight. A man can only treat us how we allow him to. Stop making excuses and make him rise to the occasion. Not only do we hurt ourselves but we also continue to hurt them. We need to speak life into our men. We need to pray for them and break strongholds and generational curses off of them. As women we need to learn how to let go of what's not holding on to us. Love yourself until God sends you someone that will love you just the way you are.

Stay Focused

The closer that you get to your breakthrough, the more the enemy will try to play tricks with you mind. Your emotions will try to creep in and remind you of how long you have been waiting for things to get better in whatever you have been walking through. Whatever you have been praying to God to change. Other people's lives seem to be going good as you're standing on the outside looking in, while your life seems the same from the inside out. It's a hard pill to swallow when all you have been doing is being nice to others, but yet they still ignore you. You have made sacrifice but your good deeds go unnoticed. You're grateful because you know that God is sitting high and counting your tear drops. While sending the Holy Spirit to comfort you. God will remind you not only of his promises to you, but when you feel like you can't take anymore he will increase himself in you and keep you grounded. God wants you to stay focused and to not worry because in due timing he will make everything right. For everything that you lost God will replace. Your breakthrough is close, continue to walk by faith and not by sight.

Hold Your Head Up

I know that times have been hard, and it's been one thing after another. You have been spending each day fighting as if it's been you against the world. Despite what's been coming toward you, God has been shielding you, protecting you against the weapons as they are being released. Holding open a door that others have told you was closed. In spite of the drought you have been lacking for nothing. Regardless of your hurt and pain, regardless of your tears, you have still been smiling in the valley. You have still been having faith in your darkest hours, because of the light that is starting to shine in you. You have been able to have joy in your soul as peace lives in your heart. The days that you didn't know how you were going to make it have been coming to pass. You have finally started embracing the beautiful woman that God created you to be. You finally realize that what God has been doing is shifting you into greatness. Change is hard especially when it is you that God is changing, it is you who old mindsets, old behaviors, old friends are disappearing. Embrace your change with open arms and keep your head up making sure that you don't miss anything that's coming your way.

Orchestrated Change

When God says move, move! Sometimes we try to bring people and things into a new season, that God is purposely trying to move you from. From around people that are actually the reason that you're still stuck in a fruitless season. People that have shown you their true color, but your heart was colorblind and ignored. We ignored people that walk away every time things get rough, but show back up once you got it under control. People that are always borrowing, but never giving. God is trying to move you from people that are holding you back from being the best version of yourself. People that don't believe in you and are only around you because of your connection with God. They have no prayer life so they want to piggyback on yours, because they don't believe in who or what they are praying for. God will move you because that's the only way that what he put in you will come to life. Open your eyes, and see people for who they truly are instead of what you have gotten accustomed to seeing. Iron sharpens iron, and when you're sharpening against something that is dull, it eventually wears, and soon it will be rendered useless. Don't resist when God is trying to move some things in your life. He is only making space for better.

The Doors to Greatness

God opens and closes doors whenever he chooses. One day you can be living what you thought was your best life, then suddenly life as you knew it changes. Leaving you confused and overwhelmed as things unravel. Your hopes, your dreams, your marriage, your friendships, your health everything is at a standstill and no matter what you are doing, you find yourself still standing and facing it alone. Nothing that you do has changed the outcome. You're drawing all your strength by hanging on to the word of God. Allowing each scripture to walk you through each day as needed. Despite everything that you're going through you continue to smile in amazement because God has been sustaining you, God has been making a way out of no way. Even though others have been speaking death, God has been fighting for you showing you that you will live. The weapons that have been sent to destroy you have been dismantled midair. While being threatened with homelessness God has been reminding you not to worry, because in his house, he has many mansions. You think of all the things that God has brought you through and your faith strengthens because you know that everything is going to be okay. You trust that everything and everyone that God removes, that he removes it for a reason and what he removes he replaces it with better. Even though God closed some doors in your life, prepare yourself because the new doors that he is about to open are doors of greatness, the best is yet to come, welcome home.

Let Go

Never second-guess or try to hold on to anyone or anything that God removes from your life. You have to realize that God will never add nor subtract anything that will interfere with you reaching your destiny. If God removes something, continue to trust his judgment and let it go. God knows a person's true intent; he knows a person's heart. Everyone that says that they are happy for you or they want the best for you, doesn't truly mean it. Some people like you because you're their go to person, you are there whenever they need you. You support them, while they are hindering you. You hear what they say about you to your face, but God hears what they say behind your back. God knows they are a priority to you but you are only an option to them. God will remove family also if they're motives aren't good. Family will stab you in the back, with the same knife that you handed them to eat with. You have caused yourself a lot of extra headaches by holding on to people that don't deserve you. Holding on to people who love and support hasn't been genuine. If God removes someone out of your life, don't get bitter or upset, because that means that God got someone else better for you, someone that will love you unconditionally for a lifetime. If someone walks away by choice, wish them the best and move on with your life, because nothing can't happen in your life without God's approval. Accept the choices and plans that God has for you. Good or bad, everything happens for a reason.

Under New Management

As you go through your daily life, remember to always take time out and thank God for everything that he has done and for everything that he is going to do for you as you continue your journey with him. No matter what, continue to stay grounded in the word of God, because the enemy will never take his target off of God's children. His attacks will start to come more frequently, and he doesn't care who or what he uses in hopes to get you to quit your journey. Keep your prayer life active, asking God to renew your strength throughout your day, because now is when you will find out who your real family and friends are. Some are going to try to discourage you from walking into your calling. Those that you thought you were close to and would always have your back, will begin to brush you off, you will begin to hear your name being drug in the dirt repeatedly. Old secrets that were once told in private will spread like wildfire. People will accuse you of acting funny or remind you constantly that you think you're better than them. Most of all prepare yourself because you will have unbelievers that don't believe the change or difference that God has made in your life. They will question your faith as they doubt your God. Instead of being grateful for the new you, they will bring up the old you. No matter what, don't let them upset you, don't let nothing separate you from the love of God, because it's not what they think about you, it's about what God thinks about you. You are under new management and under new construction. There is nothing that anyone can do to take the grace off your life or stop you from reaching your destiny.

Trust the Process

You have not faced anything in life that wasn't a part of God's plans. Rather things in your life have been good or bad in your life, it still is serving a purpose. A lot of times we want God to do things for us or give us things, but we don't want to work for it. We don't want to carry our own cross. We want the benefits, but we don't want to suffer, we don't want to wait on God's timing. We must realize that when God has something amazing for us, when our calling is greater than usual, God is going to prepare us for it before giving it to us, prepare us before revealing it. God does it not because he doesn't love us, but he wants to make sure that we can hold the size of the blessings that he's going to release to us. He wants to make sure that he can trust us with the blessings and that when we are being talked about, in him we will still trust. When people leave us, we will still be able to stand strong and make it without them. When people hurt us, we will still love them and not allow revenge to fester in our heart. God wants to know that he can still trust us when everything around us is falling apart, God wants to know that our faith in him will still remain strong. The adversities that we are facing are meant to put us in the fire so that when we come out, we will be as pure as gold, never smelling like smoke or looking like what we've been through. What you're going through might be tough, but continue to trust the process because God is going to bless you in ways that you never imagined.

1 Thessalonians 5:17 (NIRV)

Never stop praying.

The enemy uses whatever tactics necessary trying to discourage you. The enemy tries to break you mentally, in hopes that he can get you to lose faith. Get you to stop believing in the word of God. The enemy will use people on the street to push your buttons in, hoping that you will explode like a ticking time bomb. The enemy doesn't discriminate; he will use those that sit among you daily, those that you share your hopes and dreams with. He will use the ones you love to not only shatter your dreams, but to put the nails in your coffin. His intention is to kill, steal, and destroy the life that you once knew. That's why not only do you need to die daily repenting of your sins, but you also need to pray throughout your day. Praying not only for yourself, but praying for loved ones and those that you come in contact with. Praying that God will soften their heart so that they will accept him in their life and that they too could feel his abiding love. No matter how things look or what others might say, never stop praying because in due time God will part the Red Seas in your life, God will destroy your Goliaths and Pharaohs, and the tables will turn on the Judases that are in your life. Your latter days will eventually be greater than your former days. Don't get discouraged. Keep believing, and keep praying because no prayers go unheard.

The Blessing in the Test

You might be at the verge of giving up, the verge of walking away from the promises that God has given you. You may be wondering if the nonbelievers and naysayers were actually right. Are you fighting for something that's not worth the headaches? Are you believing in someone else more than they are believing in themselves? Are you going to continue walking in the season you are in, or are you going to force things to shift? When you are on a journey to greatness things are going to look messier than they are, the trials are going to bring a different level of stress, a different layer of struggle. It's going to be hard to determine your night from day. You've been planting good seeds, but you are still having a dry season. Looking for rain but no clouds in the sky. You think that maybe you remove people out of your life, because you chose to, only when you attempted to reconnect back with old friends, things no longer felt the same, so you let them go again. Old mindsets and old behaviors have faded away. So you hold on to what's left. You thank God for the few things that remain the same and the new things about yourself that are emerging. You thank God for the gifts that he placed in you that is finally coming back alive. You realize that you are stronger than what you thought. You realize that in the midst of what was meant to destroy you that you're actually growing. Even though you are going through trials, you realize that there are also blessings in the trials. So you learn everything that you need to learn to prepare yourself for your next test. Quitting is not an option.

Count It All Joy

Be prepared for your life challenges, because not every day will be a good day and every bad day, has no expiration. Like a heavy down pour you will sit patiently waiting for the rain to subside. Waiting for the wind to calm and the lightning to become nonexistent. Waiting with expectation, not knowing that in this season your forecast prediction is grey skies until further notice. You will find yourself experiencing what will be the darkest season of your life alone, and because the sky is so gray, it would be too hard to see when or if the sun would eventually shine. Alone is how you were born and for that time period alone is how you will go through that season, because nobody wants to go through the valley if they don't have to. Nobody wants to get down and dirty in a season that doesn't affect their life. Communication will become shallow and those who do decide to reach out, it's not to make sure that you're okay, but to see the damage your storm has left behind. Their physical appearance will become scarce, because they're scared that what you're going through is going to rub off on them and their situation. Your foundation will begin to crumble as fake family members and fake friends slowly disappear. As the clouds begins to lift, now in your season, you're able to evaluate and see everything else in your life that wasn't solid. There is more gone than what's left standing. All you see is unoccupied space. Suddenly while standing in despair, the Holy Spirit begins to speak and say, "Now I can use you, now that I have removed everything that has been hindering you from walking into your calling. Everything that's been taking up useless space. Everyone that's been plotting against you, everyone who was jealous of your past and whom I know are going to be envious of your future when I am done with you. Now I can use you, so instead of being hurt and angry, count it all as joy because of the seeds you have planted your harvest will be plentiful."

I Wasn't Created to Quit

There will be some things in life that come and knock you off your feet, trying to destroy your very existence while breaking the foundation that you are standing on. No matter what the situation is or what size of the Goliath you're fighting, always know that God word is unchangeable, it is alive and active and even though heaven and earth will pass away, God's word will still be here. So take refuge in God word knowing that as long as you obey him and allow him to lead your way that there will be no obstacle that you face and can't make it out of victorious. When God created us, he already knew our pass, present, and future, and he put in our path things he knew we could handle and people he knew that we needed to reach out destiny. God equipped us with the weapons that we need to fight each battle. One of our greatest weapons is faith. God didn't create us to quit, he created us to lean on him when things get hard, lean on him when we get weary. He didn't promise us that we wouldn't have problems, he promised us that he would never leave us during our problems. No matter what you're going through, always remember it's not about how many times you get knocked down, it's about making sure that you get back up after being knocked down. Some problems you don't have to defeat, your test is to outlast the opposition and not quit. Stay strong, the weapon that you need is already in you.

The Unbelievers

Not everyone will be happy or believe in the gifts that God has entrusted you with. Your talent will not be their talent, nor will their dream be yours. Don't become disappointed or discouraged in the blueprint phase of your dream. Everything that is needed to make sure that your dream come to pass God has placed in you when he gave you knowledge and wisdom. Speak life and determination in everything your heart desire. Rather you get support or not you must always believe in yourself and see the beauty that you possess in the gift that God placed in you. God has a purpose for you, and he has someone already lined up in your future to discover that dream and take you to another level. So never give up, be your biggest fan and your harvest will be plentiful. Stay strong and never stop believing.

Keep Standing

The closer that you get to your breakthrough the more the enemy will try and discourage you, in hoping that his threat of defeat and new tactics, can cause you to surrender in a battle that God has already said you won. Attacking you constantly, only because nothing the enemy has used to try and destroy you in the past has worked. The enemy is standing in a state of shock. A state of confusion knowing that they have took you through hell, but you don't look like what you been through. They have tossed you in the furnace, but you don't smell like smoke. They have left you for dead, but still you rise. You have been singled out by the kiss of Judas, but Jesus paid the price. The enemy is trying to figure out how you are still standing, when they knocked you down, why you are smiling, when they stripped you from the life you once knew, how can you still have joy in a time of chaos. I got it because greater is he, who is in me and through him all things are possible. So I am going to stand firm in my faith, knowing that no weapons formed shall prosper. Because God has the final say so. No matter what, keeping standing, because God is standing with you.

Don't Get Discouraged

See, I am doing a new thing! Now it springs up;
do you not perceive it? I am making a way in the
wilderness and streams in the wasteland. (Isaiah
43:19 NIV)

You may be at a point in your life, that your mind is in a million places right now, you're wondering how you're going to make it, while still trying to figure out how did you get there. Defeat is bravely knocking at your door, while answering is not an option, only because you don't have enough strength to do so. You're contemplating about letting others know what you are going through, but the disappointment of them not being able to help, encourages you to keep it to yourself. You're trying to handle everyday life situations, while taking care of your family and everyone else, yet barely taking care of yourself. We are not superwoman, every battle wasn't made for us to fight, so instead of stressing yourself out, concentrate on the word of God knowing that he will never leave you or forsake you. Press your way through this difficult moment knowing that this too shall pass. God knows what you are going through and not only is he turning things around in your favor, but he is also opening new doors of opportunity, new doors of favor and new doors of blessings and new doors of breakthrough. Be strong knowing that the Lord will provide.

Matthew 7:3 (NIV)

Why do you look at the speck of sawdust in your
brother's eye and pay no attention to the plank in
your own eye?

We as woman go around pointing out flaws in others, laughing
at their downfalls, finding humor in their pain, yet never acknowl-
edging that we are not flawless. We go through life blaming others
for our difficulties, and bad breaks never considering what we did to
contribute to it. We allow putting others down, to become our kryp-
tonite in picking us up. Everyone of us have been hurt in one way
or another, or we deal with emotional baggage that hold us bound
because we haven't cast them away. Even though we were created
by God, we are not perfect, flesh and sin has made us imperfect.
We will never be able to come together in unity as woman, because
we are the ones tearing each other down. Take a moment and look
at yourself, ask God to search your heart and to remove everything
that is not pleasing in his sight. Accept your faults and find ways to
improve you, so that once God transform you with the renewing of
your mind, you will be able to encourage someone else instead of
discouraging them. Remember it is our imperfections that make us
beautiful.

Lost

Not realizing until the damage is done, we go through life walking in the shadows of men who don't love us, continuously trying to please them by becoming who they want us to be, while losing ourselves in the process. We have allowed ourselves to be up on a pedestal when the one who placed us there out of arrogance isn't qualified to have who they are trying to create, but yet we stay. Allowing our self-esteem to be lowered, changing our appearance, while letting someone else dictate how our story ends, in their fantasy but our reality. We focus on being who they want us to be at the expense of losing who we were born to be. We become a broken woman, at the hands of a broken man who is using us by trying to fill a void and misplaced anger from his childhood. We take the abuse for a problem we didn't create. We become emotional punching bags, for the boy that is still trapped inside of the man's body, all because he was starved of the one thing he wanted and needed as a child, his mother's love. That's when we have to realize that we can't heal a man that won't admit he has a problem. It's not because we don't love them, but it's because his mother is someone we will never be and he has to forgive her, before we can forgive him, if not you will spend the rest of your life being punished and trying to fix something you had no control over. Always remember that hurt people can only hurt people. Save yourself or you'll lose yourself in the shadows.

Romans 8:25 (AMPC)

But if we hope for what is still unseen by us, we
wait for it with patience and composure.

You may have been praying to God about somethings that haven't come to past or with the natural eye you haven't saw manifesting, so you start talking yourself out of the relationship improving, out of opening the business, out of your health getting better, out of the blessings of God because you have become discouraged while waiting. When praying we need to always remember that God do things in his timing and not ours, just like flowers, if what we are asking God for or to do is given in the wrong season of our life, like a flower we will not grow. We also must take into consideration that the seed we sown may be the reason we aren't harvesting. God holds us back a lot of times to teach us patience, to grow our faith in him, and to birth something out of us. In your time of despair, don't concentrate on the seen but thank him in advance for what he is doing behind the scenes. Some of God's blessings must be performed on the inside of us, in our situation for God to get his greatest glory on the outside. So even though what you are facing is uncomfortable, we are only delayed but not denied from our blessing.

James 1:17 (ESV)

Every good gift and every perfect gift is from
above, coming down from the Father of lights,
with whom there is no variation or shadow due
to change

In us, God has placed many gifts
Gifts that are waiting on us to birth
In some of us, gifts have already been reviled
We just didn't understand they're worth

We have allowed others to speak over us
Telling us who we can or cannot be
Their unbelief in us has been holding us back
When through him, God said we were free

Even though you may have pushed your gift aside, the value in
it has not decrease. Accept your gift with grace.

God Is Waiting

No matter what you might be going through, just know that you are not alone. God has been waiting on you to decide that you want better and for once to mean it. God has been waiting on you to admit that you need him every hour of the day. Like me, you probably have been going through life only coming to God whenever you needed him to open a door, whenever you needed him to fix something, heal somebody or to make a way out of no way, because you've messed up again. Like clockwork, I was coming faithfully, putting in my prayer request as needed. Even though God knew that I was playing a dangerous game, God still covered me. God loved me enough to see me through every situation that I faced, despite all the times that I kept walking out of God's alignment, he was still there. For years I pretended I was going to change, yet I was coming and going as I pleased, until finally God said enough. God called my name and my life has never been the same. Don't get me wrong, it wasn't easy in the beginning, because I was way off course, and God had to bring me back to reality by allowing me to experience a season full of adversities. During that season, not only did I find myself, but most of all, I found God. As each day passes, the more I fall in love with God. I have no regrets other than wishing that I would have acknowledged his presence sooner. God has done some amazing things in my life and I thank him for the favor he has on my life. You may think that there are some chains and habits that you can't break, but all you have to do is surrender, and God will do the rest. God is waiting on you and loves you and said come as you are. He's waiting!

Pray Your Way Out

When we are going through situations, sometimes our mind gets caught up in the moment and we feel pressed. Friends and family with no or little faith try to wear us down with words of defeat. They try to convince us that what we have been praying for isn't coming to pass. They hope that in our waiting stage of God prevailing and restoring marriages, restoring financial stability, healing our health needs or the turning around of our disobedient kids is not going to happen, because we have been in the storm for a while. Despite what others may say, continue to stand on God's words, refusing to make a permanent decision in a temporary situation. Continue praying and wait with expectations knowing that God is going to turn things around. Continue to hold your head up knowing if God allowed what you're going through to happen, that God also planned an exit for you and that you're in your waiting season. God will allow us to sit in that waiting season to teach us patience, to show us that even though others might have left us battling the storm alone, that he is still with us sleeping on the bottom of the boat. He will not steer us wrong and will calm our seas and the winds in due time. Regardless of those standing ashore waiting on your demise, stand strong, because while they are waiting to see what happens to you, God is doing something magnificent to them on the inside. Seasons shifts and situations change, so continue to have faith and pray your way out as you press your way through.

Stay Faithful in the Moment

No matter what you are going through, regardless of how many times you have been knocked over or put down, despite how many tears you have shed, or how bad the trauma may be, being faithful in the moment matters. God allows us to go through things to see if in the midst of our chaos, in the midst of us being mistreated, in the midst of us being talked about, in the midst of others walking away and in the midst of being betrayed, God wants to know if in our darkest moment, will we be faithful in that moment. God wants to know if we will still praise him, will we still be kind to those who have hurt us, will we forgive with an unconditional heart, will we still serve him and continue to walk in our calling with grace. A lot of times because things are not going how we want them to or our situations aren't shifting as quickly as we had hoped for, we get frustrated and our faithfulness starts to waver, we stop showing up how we were created to be and allow the old us to creep back in. God allows us to go through things because God wants to know if he can trust us, he wants to know when he releases the things that we ask him for or to do in our life, we will still give all glory to him in the moment we are in. Will we still acknowledge him? Despite the times that we have walked away, God has never left us nor forsaken us. Stay faithful in the moment and watch God turn things around for you in the moment you are in.

Self-Care

We spend our life trying to be superheroes, trying to be everything that others need, pouring and pouring to the point that we have nothing left to pour. We comfort others and tell them that they are going to be okay, when emotionally we are falling apart. Secretly we find ourselves drowning but our head is still above water. No matter how things look, we continue to hang on praying that better days are coming. We neglect ourselves constantly, just so others can have. We have moments when "You can do it" is standing at the front door, but defeat is knocking at the back door. We experience sleepless nights, that eventually leads to countless nights where our eyes are closed but our minds are still open, holding conversations with ourselves that we can't discuss with others. We experience moments when tears flow out of our eyes like a river, but it still doesn't resolve our pain. We are only standing because we don't have anyone that we can depend on to pick us up. We as women have to start showing up for ourselves. We must start making sure that we are okay, heart, mind, body, and soul. God created us in his image and our footsteps have already been ordered, so just because we are women he didn't create us to live in a world of chaos by trying to be everything that others need. God wants us to cast all our burdens on him so that we can start taking care of ourselves. Rest in God's arms and allow him to rest in your heart.

Walk by Faith and Not by Sight

When you continue to stand on the word of God, there is nothing that anyone can say that can stop you from receiving the blessings that God has for you or interfere with the calling that God has on your life. You might have been stuck in your season for a while, but God said don't faint or get weary, don't give in because your breakthrough is coming. Don't stress over a battle that is already won in the spirit realm. Nothing that you have gone through in life has happened by chance. Every trial that you have been fighting was needed to get you to your destiny. Even though you were disappointed during the process, you will be blessed through the purpose, so instead of wondering why, thank God for those who walked away, for those who betrayed you, for those who slandered your name, for those who left you for dead, thank God for the good and the bad, because it was all a part of God's plan. Not only to strengthen your faith, and take you to another level, but to also get the glory from others. God's word says that he will use your enemies to bless you and what was meant for bad, will be used for good. So get prepared because God is about to bless you abundantly for the tears you shed, the things you lost, the sleepless nights, everything that you have gone through, God said count it all joy. So even though others have counted you out, God said continue to stand, because it's not over. Don't get in agreeance with the naysayers or unbelievers, continue to speak life over your situation and in your situation. Continue to trust in God to deliver you. Continue to believe that all things work together for good to them that love the Lord, to them who are called according to his purpose.

In Due Time

I would like to encourage you that in due time, your fog will lift and your season will begin to shift. For months or years, your heart has been constantly broken. Hurt by people that you thought would be prospering with you, people that you thought you would be sharing this important moment in your life together, but God saw differently. God showed you that you had outgrown some people, others were dead weight, so now you only have memories of what once was while staying focused on what's to be, while transforming into the beautiful woman God created you to be. You realize now that meeting that person is more important than who you used to be. Even though you have found yourself being on this journey alone, you continue to lean on the word of God, because you know that this was all a part of God's plans and better is coming. You comfort yourself with God's words knowing that even though the weapons will form, you know that he won't let anything hurt you. despite everything that you have lost, you hold on to knowing that weeping may endure for the night but joy comes in the morning. You remind yourself that your latter days will be greater than your former days. What you're experiencing hurts, but you accept that all of it was a part of God's plan, rather good or bad it all is contributing to the woman you're becoming. Look at your progress, you have come too far to give up now. You're closer than you think and will reach your destination in due time, hold on.

Proverbs 29:21 (NIV/MSG)

A servant pampered from youth, will turn to be insolent. If you let people treat you like a door-mat, you'll be quite forgotten in the end

I spent a lot of my life pleasing others, not realizing that not only was I neglecting myself; I was opening up the door to how I would allow others to treat me. Regardless of how nasty I had been treated, disrespected, talked about, put down and let down, I was faithfully catering to others needs. I was trying to make sure they were okay when I was the one hurt and betrayed. I put myself in the position to be abused for unknown reasons, but yet I was the one apologizing. I was the one opening back up the lines of com-munication of fighting to save relationships, when all the lines that could be broken were broken. Still I fought. I was there for people in friendships that I knew were talking about me behind my back, but yet I was still being loyal, when my ears were burning. I have protected others trying to help them save their job, but yet they were throwing me under the bus. I have put myself in situations where I have helped people out financially, but they left me hanging when I was in need. I have bent over backward for many, but at this moment in my life standing beside me are very few. Despite everything that I went through I hold no grudges, because without them I wouldn't be the woman I am today. I learned my lesson the hard way. But I am thankful I was blessed to see who my true friends are.

Matthew 14:28–29 (NIV)

"Lord, if it's you," Peter replied, "tell me to come to you on the water." Jesus replied, "Come."

God has placed beautiful dreams in you, dreams that you may think are impossible or too big for you to visualize, but God chose you to give birth to that dream, he knew that you were the woman for the job, he knew that despite what you're going through and what you been through, he knew that you could do it, because those dreams are attached to your destiny. They are dreams that as long as you stay focused you will achieve. On your journey to your destiny, you will face a lot of adversities and a lot of things that will try and distract you in hopes to get you off course, in hopes that the sweet whispers of "You can't do it" will cloud your judgment and will replace the voice of God. Replace him reassuring you that he equipped you with everything you need for this journey. There will be people that try and discourage you in hopes to shake your faith and have you revert back to the old you. The angry you, the weak and vulnerable you. Regardless of how things look, regardless of the battle that you are facing, always remember that God has the final say and not only can he move mountains, but he can soften hearts, and with one touch of favor he can and will turn your situation around. Stay focused on what God told you and you will make it to the promised land.

1 Corinthians 7:23 (NKJV)

You were bought with a price; do not become slaves of men.

You may feel that you're going through life weighed down by things you did in your past. You're living in chaos because you can't live in peace. Constantly being whipped, not because you don't forgive yourself, but because others don't forgive you. You are trying to make up for past mistakes that others won't allow you to live down. You have been jumping through hoops and losing sleep day in and day out, trying to get back on someone's good side, but yet they're abusing you with their bad side. Silently you're enduring it, because you feel that you deserve it. Unforgiveness has cost many people to go to their graves in turmoil, never forgiving or being forgiven, I'm sorry no longer matters in a dead situation. You can't move forward, because you are being held hostage by someone who is using unforgiveness as a form of punishment. Some people have done things wrong in parenthood, relationships and friendships, but yet the betrayal is a constant reminder and the burden is still being carried. Even though God's word says that time waits for no man, time is still not considered valuable enough for one to forgive and forget. That's why you have to realize there is nothing that you can do to change a person with a hardened heart, take them to God in prayer stop beating yourself up and live in peace because the price has already been paid.

Don't Get Comfortable Being Comfortable

Everything that we go through in life has a purpose, and regardless of what that purpose is, it will never decrease the value in the lesson to be learned. A lot of times we focus on what we're going through instead of why we are going through it. We don't meditate on the areas of our lives that need to be improved or weakness in us that need to be strengthen. Instead, we get upset with the timing, that purpose chose to teach us.

Some of us have doors that need to be closed yet were holding them open afraid of change. There are doors that have been opened, but we won't walk through because of fear. We allow people to take up residence in our daily life never questioning their motives, but never paying attention to what progress has been made since occupancy was obtained. We sit at jobs for years, never leaving a mark of appreciation, only a stain of remembrance. We settle with enough, because having more means we have to do more, so even though we believe it, we don't want to put in the work to achieve it. God allows us to face adversities because being uncomfortable is the only way that we will move out of comfortable.

> And the God of all grace, who called you to his external glory in Christ, after you have suffered a little while, will himself restore you and make you strong, firm and steadfast. (1 Peter 5:10 NIV)

Proverbs 16:9 (ESV)

The heart of man plans his way, but the Lord
establish his steps

You will deal with a lot of people in life who will try and convince you how your story will end. They will try to get you to give up on things that you are still praying to God for. They will try to cause doubt in things that you are still trusting God to do. They will slander your name with lies and discredit your character. Holding on to your past and refusing to acknowledge your present. They will attack everything about you. Regardless of what they say in hopes to break you, in hopes they can hurt you, in hopes to prove that they control the outcome of your life and the success of your hopes and dreams. Continue to trust in God. Continue to keep on walking into your calling. Don't waste your time trying to prove them wrong, because in due time God will reveal himself to them as well. You can't stop a person from voicing their opinion nor change how they feel in their heart, but we serve a God who can and who will in his timing.

Deuteronomy 31:6 (NLT)

So be strong and courageous! Do not be afraid
and do not panic before them. For the Lord your
God will personally go ahead of you. He will
never fail you nor abandon you.

Some journeys that you take in life are meant for you to walk
alone. Trusting in God to direct your path. Regardless of how sincere a person sounds or try to convince you that they have your best
interest at heart, only stand firm on the word of God, because he is
a God that cannot lie.

The intentions of the heart belong to man, but
the answer of the tongue comes from the Lord.
(Proverbs 16:1 NET)

You will never know the true motives behind a person's actions
or what's hiding in a person's heart, until you're put in a situation
and the mouth begins to speak what the heart truly feels. While
you're thanking God for your uprising, they are silently praying for
your downfall, because envy and jealousy hides behind pride, which
is enforced by hate. All because the heart let down its guard and
allowed someone to speak five lies that Satan uses to discourage us.

I can't
God won't
Nobody cares
I don't matter
It's too late

No matter what you are facing right now, always remember that God allowed it to happen, because it must happen for the season, he is getting ready to shift you into. So stand strong and be courageous, the best is yet to come. God's timing is perfect.

James 4:2 (NIV)

You do not have because you do not ask God.

A lot of times the scripture "You have not because you ask not" is easily spoken, but not understood and when not understood you will lose faith and walk out of the alignment of God because of your lack of knowledge about God. When praying to God about silent battles you are fighting, circumstances that you want him to fix, gifts that you want to be given, storms that you want him to cease or Goliaths that you want to be removed, you must make sure that your heart is pure, and your motives are not deceitful. Our vision of what lies ahead, is perceived on how far we can see with the naked eye, instead of what God has already seen with his spiritual eye. So just because we asked God to do something doesn't mean he will answer in the way that we were expecting him to. Sometimes not answering is the best answer. God is a righteous God, and he will not release things into your atmosphere that will interfere with the journey to your destination. God will not release something that brings death to you, when it is not your appointed time. God will not release something that obtaining it is only out of greed and pride, when sustaining it you will not be able to handle, because of the wisdom you lack. Most of all, God will not release anything that is not in his will or out of his timing or control. Even in your disappointments, rejoice and know that there is a time for everything.

Don't Be Dismayed

I know that it may seem as if you have been stuck in a season that won't shift. Even though the sun has begun to rise, your visibility has been impaired by a fog that won't lift. Faithfully you have been praying and waiting on God to move, but the only thing that seems to be moving is people walking in and out of your life. It appears to be a different day, but the same burdens that you're caring. Weariness has started to take on residence in your thoughts and now your mind is being held captive by confusion. Due to only unknown predictions on when your situation will come to pass, you're unsure if this is the way that God intended for your story to end or if out of fear you have skipped chapters and jumped to conclusions. Even though giving up was never an option, you wonder that now might be your best interest. I am here to reassure you that regardless of what your situation may look like, always remember that your thoughts are not God thoughts, nor is your ways God's ways. Don't determine your survival off your opinion but determine it off the word of God and his promises. In your trying times continue to stand and look to the mountains where your help will come from. Realize that what you are facing is a part of the plan to your destiny. It's not meant for you to try and figure out why you're going through it or how you're going to make it through it. The test is to strengthen you and your faith when he brings you through it. So continue to lean not on your own understanding but to trust in God, your breakthrough is coming.

The New You

Regardless of your imperfections, never give up or limit yourself on becoming the woman that God created you to be. Never give up on your hopes and dreams, just to live in someone else's shadow. God placed something unique in you, something that only you can discover, only you can set the value, and only you can activate. Despite what your today looks like, concentrate on your tomorrow, knowing that this too shall pass, because God is in control and all things work together for our good. Be still and know that he is God, lean not on your own understanding, but trust in him with all your heart, and he will direct your path. So never allow the new you not to take root and grow, because of the detachments the old you must let go of. Never get comfortable with being enough, when deep down you know that you deserve better. Never get comfortable with descending, when like an eagle God created you to soar.

Life is too short, so never live it through the eyes of someone else, when your vision for yourself is so much clearer. God will prune you and things around you, so the woman you have been holding captive can emerge.

Jeremiah 29:11 (NIV)

"For I know the plans I have for you," declares the Lord, "plans to prosper you and not harm you, plans to give you hope and a future."

He's Ready

Before you were born, God planted something in you. Something unique so that you would stand out, instead of fit in. Something meant for you to shine and rise above, instead of dimming your light and playing it safe in below. Something wonderful, but still hidden, protected by fear instead of believing in faith. That fear of believing has allowed you to walk with comfort, in the limited words spoken over your life "declaring this is how your story end", but God said, the day you hear my voice harden not your heart, because this is where your true story begin.

He's Knocking

You have been running for years avoiding your calling, but faithfully God has been behind you every step of the way. Never forsaking you nor leaving you, only waiting on you patiently to pray. You have been going through life doing things your way, but despite your disobedience, God covered you with his grace.

Will You Answer

God is waiting on you to put your trust in him and allow him to direct your path because he has so much more for you. Will you finally believe and walk with him by faith.

Before It's Too Late

Reason for Your Season

God allows things to happen in our lives to shake us up, not only because he sees greater in us, but a lot of times we take him and the things that he has given us or done for us, for granted. We come to him faithfully when we need a blessing, but once he releases it into the atmosphere, once he removes it, once he fixes it, we step out of the grace of God, back into the world of the ungodly. Thinking that we got everything under control, thinking that we can fight our battles without the help of him or without putting on the full armor of God and wearing it daily. God knows the plans he has for us, and he will allow whatever adversities to come our way to strengthen us in areas of our life and areas of our faith that need to be increased to fulfill his purpose. God will allow us to go through the fire until everything that is hindering us is burned off. Our season won't shift, until fear is burned off, until abandonment is burned off, until hate is burned off, until grudges are burned off. Until doubt is burned off, until repeating the same cycle is burned off. God's plan is to prosper us and not harm us. Even though God takes and keeps us in the fire, rest assured with knowing you are not alone. During your waiting seasons you have to continue to trust God and remember that all things work together for his good and when you least expect it your seasons will shift and you will walk into your calling more gracefully. Your Season has a Reason.

I Will Praise You in the Rain

I have faced so many challenging things in my life, things that were meant to kill me, things that were meant to break me, things that shook my life off of its very foundation leaving only memories of its existence and visions of what could be, if I humbly submit and allow God to have his way. Before I was transformed with the renewing of my mind, I was looking at things with the natural eye instead of the spiritual eye. I was allowing my problems to take my focus off of God. I was trying to fix my problems alone instead of leaning on the Lord for his guidance and understanding. Only making problems worse in a world of no remorse. Never realizing that what I was going through was all a part of God's divine plan, a plan that without his intervention I would never develop into who he said I was and can be. If it wasn't for God saving me, I would have never got to feel God's abiding love. I would never get to see his magnificent hand in my life. I would never be able to acknowledge his presence and thank him for all the times he spared my life. God has been amazing to me and no matter what I face I will never lose my faith in him. I will praise him in the rain.

I Wasn't Born to Quit

The God we serve sits high and looks low, never sleeping, only keeping a watchful eye over our joy, over our peace, over our life and over our salvation. Like a thief in the middle of the might, the enemy has been lurking, hungrily waiting to try to find anything that he can use to attack us, in hoping that we would turn our back on the God that we serve and abort our mission, abort our calling and abort our trust in God. You have come to far from where you started from, and God has brought you through too much to walk away now. Regardless of the threats on your life, continue to stand firm vowing I will not surrender, I will continue to trust that God will reveal himself in every situation that I'm facing, and he will make my enemies my footstool. God sees what you're going through, and he will use the same people that slandered your name to speak life into every dream that you envision. He will bless you in the presence of your enemy. You might be bruised, but you are not broken, hurt but not surprised. You have fought one battle after another, but you continued to fight. Continue to fight because your breakthrough is near. For every tear that you have shed in sorrow, in due time you will reap in joy. For every lie and betrayal that's been told, every tongue shall confess. In due time your season will shift, but until then continue to praise God in your winter, because movement generates heat and heat creates friction, friction creates fire and where there is fire, there will also be smoke. Help is on the way. Stay strong you weren't built to quit.

Wear Your Crown Gracefully

You will experience moments in your life that you find yourself making decisions not because it is what your heart desire or judgement made by what is best for you, but because you have allowed someone or something to dictate the silent voice that openly wants to be heard but have been forced closed, led to believe that there are no more options.

So You Give In

You have been making life decisions enforce by what they say, instead of what God said. You have been standing at doors that you never entered because you assumed was locked. Your effort to grow was doomed with failure, because it was based off someone with a no effort to try mentality.

So You Give Up

You have limited what you can have, by what others do not want to see you with. You have been sabotaging you dreams for the future, with things spoken in the past. You have been diming your light, just so someone else could shine, who has no vision. You have been trying to fit in when God created you to stand out. You are a queen who was chosen and whose life was predestined by God. It might have slipped before, but the time has come, adjust your crown, embrace yourself and be proud of who you are.

Bruised but Not Broken

Hey, You

Always remember that no matter what you are going through, it will never be bigger than our God:

Believe

You can do all things through Christ who strengthens you:

Trust

Do not allow things that was created to be simple, to become complicated:

Breathe

Fear and doubt will always be around the corner waiting to step in:

Prepare

You are beautiful, intelligent, and wonderfully made:

Smile

No matter how busy your day may get, always remember to:

Pray

In the Fire

The more we walk with Christ, we will begin to realize the more adversities we will face. We will experience seasons that will feel like winter, while everyone else is enjoying spring. We will experience downpours and torrential rains, while others see not a cloud in the sky. Our days will be long, as far as the east is from the west because sleepless nights, is still considered our day. People that we love, and we thought we could trust, will be as deceitful as those we have never known. We will face times that all we will see is the backs of others, as they close the door forever to "I'm here if you need me." What once was, is now gone, and what is gone, you never had.

Alone you will feel for forty day and forty nights, drifting in the sea of confusion, realizing that you spent your former days pouring into others, yet you are floating alone. You think about your visions and dream that never took root, because you were busy watering someone else grass. Showing constant support but getting no love in return, only being scorched under their sun. Your well ran dry, because you were quenching thirst, now you are severely dehydrated drifting alone.

As you are in this moment of your life, pay attention to your surroundings and realize that when God got a purpose for you and a calling on your life, he will do whatever he needs to do to prepare you for it. God had to get you there, to get you here, right where he can use you.

> Pure gold put in the fire comes out of it proved pure: genuine faith put through this suffering comes out proved genuine. When Jesus wraps this all up, it is your faith, not your gold, that God will have on display as evidence of his victory. (1 Peter 1:7 MSG)

Staying Content in Your Season

A lot of times we go through things in our life and we pray to God to fix it, we pray to him to change circumstances and often times we pray for God to change people and because he don't change it when we want him to or within the time frame we expected him to do it, sometimes we get discouraged and in our place of discouragement we step out of God alignment and we try to handle things ourself. In that moment of discouragement, we switch up our prayer life and instead of concentrating on who is with us during the storm, we begin to focus on the size of the storm and while looking at the size of the storm, we allow doubt and fear to creep in and have us wonder if we could weather the storm.

We begin to look at the things that the storm has uprooted, until we do not see the things that are starting to take root, we focus on how many days and nights it has been raining in our storm, until we do not notice that even though we have been beaten and battered that we are still afloat despite the storm. We worry about the valleys that is drenched with flooded waters, until we do not notice the dry land that is starting to recede beyond the water. We worry about the things we lost, instead of wondering about the jewels unearthed. We worry more about the people that we asked God to change, until we do not notice the speck that is in our eye, because the thorn that is in our side has begun to take our focus from God promises.

Instead of looking up toward the heavens, we begin to look down at the earth, not realizing that now by looking down we start to see things that we do not want to step in, so we start to step over, we see things and people that are passing us by, so we pick up our pace and begin to rush. We forget about the little things, because the big things are more appealing, but most of all we get our roses confused with our weeds so we cut what should had only been pruned, and destroy the possibility for potential.

During our storms, we make permanent decisions, in temporary situations, forgetting that in God's word he told us in Ecclesiastes 3:1–11, "There is a time for everything, and a season for every activity under the sun." He was letting us know that we are going to have some good days and some bad days, but he also reassured us that even if we experience those times, that not only did he create them for a purpose, but he went before us to make sure that we would be able to make it through. God also told us in in Psalm 30:5, "Weeping may endure for a night, but joy cometh in the morning." So in your storm it may be uncomfortable and confusing, but in due time the season will shift, and the Glory of God will be revealed. Stay strong and trust in the our Heavenly Father who can do all things but fail.

Ecclesiastes 3:11 (NKJV)

He has made everything beautiful in its time.

Despite your upbringing or your past, never doubt yourself or the person that God created you to be. Sometimes we allow the words that has been spoken over us as a child or things that happened to us throughout the years to hinder us from prospering, hindering us from who God created us to be before placing us in our mother's womb. We feel that we can't be great due to the things we were lacking or not introduce to. We must understand that God has a plan and a timing for everything under the sun. Some of us were created to transition in a caterpillar stage, because what God put in us needs time to grow and we need time to experience things, so that once our time comes, we will blossom into a beautiful butterfly. God hold none of the things that we did prior or present over our head, he forgives us from all our sins when we come to him with a heart of repentance. From this day forward you should start to forgive yourself too. Release the burdens that you have been carrying, release your mistakes and look at them as learning lessons. So that you will be able to encourage someone else. You wouldn't have a testimony if you or your faith in God had not been put to a test. Ask God to guide your footsteps and you will blossom into your calling.

Ephesians 4:31 (NKJV)

Let all bitterness and wrath and anger and clamor
and slander be put away from you, along with all
malice.

The time has come for you to release the anger and bitterness
that you have been holding on to. Rather you are holding on to hurt
and pain caused by a loved one or something or someone that you
encountered in your daily life. Holding on to it has only hurt you
because you haven't been enjoying the life God intended for you to
have. You have wasted countless days of your time contemplating
getting even or wishing bad on someone and there off living their
best life. You're dwelling on them, when you have never crossed their
mind. We don't know, nor will we ever know the true intentions in
a person heart or why they said or did something spiteful to us. We
hope that a person apologizes, but then if they did, if our heart has
hardened, we would wonder if it was sincere or straight out say that
we don't forgive them. The bible tells us to forgive them and love
them just as Christ has done the same for us. They talked about Jesus
and instead of him allowing it to hinder him, he continued his journey and that is what you need to do. Don't get stuck in the past and
allow it to affect your future. Let go and allow God to handle them,
because no matter what they have done it will not affect the promises
or life that God has for you. Only you can stop it by standing still,
move on and allow the joy in you to shine.

Ecclesiastes 3:6 (NKJV)

A time to keep and a time to throw away.

When God removes a person out of our life, it hurts because we are human and have gotten attached to being around or living with the person that God removed, so just like we grieve the death of someone we care about, we also grieve the detachment part of a friendship or a relationship that we must let go of. The difference is we try to hold on to the things that aren't physically dead. We spend years trying to be who we are not, years giving eighty and settling for twenty. Years of allowing ourselves to endure some type of abuse at the expense of the person God is trying to remove. When God speaks or steps in to direct our path, we need to humbly submit, because if they were a part of our destiny and needed along our journey, they would be there. God knows who and what we need an when a person is removed it's because God has something better for us. We hold ourselves back but then complain about how many years we wasted or was miserable in a relationship. When we were never physically bound. When we are no longer producing good fruit, and the time has come for our season to shift, we will shift but what wasn't meant to go with us will not. Stop holding on to people that's not actively holding on to you, stop making them a priority in your life when we are only and option in theirs. We outgrow our childish ways; we outgrow clothes, and we outgrow relationships also. The detachment phase is temporary. God is preparing you for greater.

Humble Yourself

We as women must manage our emotions better. A lot of times, we speak without listening. We react when there was no significant reason for us to act, only to acknowledge that we heard what was being said. We don't have to like it, but we do have to respect it especially pertaining to matters of the heart. We try to be our mate's mother, when a mother is not what they need. A friend is not who they need. What our mate needs is to feel that he can trust us with his feelings, trust that pillow talk remains pillow talk between each other. No matter what might be going on, he needs us to always show him respect as a man and treat him like a man. Rather he is going through baby mama drama, health issues, financial issues, or everyday life issues. We have female friends that we can relate to if we need to vent, but our mate doesn't have that, because sometimes what he might disclose risk the chance of being brought back up during a football game or playing cards with a group of others, so they hold it in. Dealing with it however they can. We never know what our mate is going through or what past insecurities he might be dealing with. Our job is to listen, support and love our mate through it. Yes, they might tell us it's nothing, or they don't want to talk about it, but during being there for them, also allow them their space to breathe, allow them their time to vent. Don't make them feel that they can't talk to you, because they will shut down and that line of communication can only be opened through prayer and God intervening and softening their heart. Take your problems to God because only he can give your mate strength when he is weak.

Cast Your Stone

A lot of things in life, we give up on, before ever reaching our potential. Things that were not denied only delayed. Precious things that our heart desired, and things that our creator set aside for us. Instead of having the best, we accept good enough. Yet our soul is still thirsty, still hungry, and still got a burning flame, fear came and whispered "You cannot do it," while faith stood there quietly but firmly.

Faith watched you make one bad choice after another. Faith watched you get over looked at jobs continuously. Faith watched the bad example that you were setting for your kids. Faith watched you agree to what the heart did not want. Faith watched your dreams pass you by. Faith watched the countless nights that you tossed and turned because your mind was not at peace. Faith watched while fear slept comfortably within.

Faith watched, because it knew that until you evict fear out of your life (Romans 12:2), and conform any longer to the pattern of the world, but be transformed by the renewing of your mind, then fear will always lay dormant until the next opportunity present itself. Fear will always sabotage your vision and interfere with your tomorrows. Fear will always whisper even when nobody is around to hear it. Fear feed itself in silence and dwells in darkness. Like David in 1 Samuel 17:49, with a sling and one stone you can defeat every goliath in your life. All it takes is the faith of a mustard seed. Now be brave. *Cast your stone!*

New Beginning

There will be moments in your life that will make you question your very existence. As you are sitting alone in frustration without an ounce of hope in your eye, your mind will begin to wonder "Is this really the life intended for me?" You have noticed that everything in your life that could go wrong, has went wrong. Blood is no longer thicker than water, and water has now run dry. Daily you dread living life because the thought of what is next is lurking like a thief in broad daylight. While you are trying to figure out how you are going to make it, "next" shows its ugly face and that moment has switched into a new gear called "You just cannot take it." Mentally and emotionally, you have been drained. You are going to war internally with no strength to fight externally, only showing up because somewhere is better than nowhere, yet deep down defeat is whispering, at the place you are in, they both feel the same. Sitting in self-pity only begins to anger you as you watch others gleefully pass you by, busy making plans for tomorrow when you are still stuck in today.

At that very moment, you utter into the atmosphere "God save me," and a warm sensation rushes through your body. The Holy Spirit begins to speak. Romans 10:13 says, "For everyone who calls on the name of the Lord will be saved." Psalm 50:15 says, "Call upon me in the day of trouble; I will deliver thee and thou shalt glorify me." We read in Hebrews 13:5, "I will never leave thee nor forsake thee." Jeremiah 29:11 tells us, "'For I know the plans I have for you,' declares the Lord, 'plans to prosper you and not harm you, plans to give you hope and a future.'" Proverbs 3:5–6 tells us, "Trust in the Lord with all your heart and lean not on your own understanding; in all your ways submit to him." My friend, you have been living your life outside of the will of God. You have been doing things your way and not God's way. Surrender to him and let him guide your footsteps. In due time, he will make your crooked roads straight. Today is the first day of the rest of your life, because you are now in the potter's hand, and he is working in your favor.

Hold On

Life has probably knocked you down a few times and getting back up slowly starts to take its toll, instead of stopping to see if you are okay, life continues full speed, with time never stopping only pieces of debris blowing in the wind, reminding you that someone else has traveled that path before you. The road you are on may seem difficult to endure, but it is still safe to travel.

We must always remember that despite what we go through in life, "the Lord himself goes before you and will be with you; he will never leave you nor forsake you. Do not be afraid; do not be discouraged" (Deuteronomy 31:8).

We are going to face adversities and experience seasons that may seem to have stood still. We will have burdens, that often time carrying will seem to be more than we could bare. We will face times that put us on our back and when those times come stay looking up. Even during those times that you cannot stand, continue to kneel in prayer. Pray without ceasing, believing that your breakthrough is near.

What you are experiencing is only a test. A test that in your former years you have already been equipped for. Revisit those moments in your life, pull strength from those times, pull joy from those times, pull moments of peace from those times, to evaporate the chaos. Strengthen your faith by looking at those situations and remember that if God brought you through it before, then he is the same God that will do it again. Comfort your anxiety with the thought of knowing that God did not put you in this situation, without knowing how or when he was going to bring you out of it.

Psalm 31:15 tells us that at the right time, God will provide your need. At the right time God will deliver you. At the right time, God will rescue you. Hold on and be strong.

Spoken Words

A lot of times we self-sabotage ourselves, not because we choose failure, but because we allow the things that has been spoken over us to hinder us from who God created us to be before ever placing us into the womb of our mother (Jeremiah 1:5). What should had been a path to generational blessings, becomes an ongoing generational curse if not broken.

So often we tend to forget that there is power in the tongue (Proverbs 18:21). We can speak life or death into any situations. Into our hopes, our dreams, our kids, our marriage like a poisonous venom our words can soak in and penetrate one's heart and mind instantly, before ever having the opportunity to give birth to potential, give birth to possibilities, give birth to the plans that God have for us (Jeremiah 29:11).

Without hesitation, we speak things out of anger, out of jealousy. And most of the time, out of disappointment that we carry around daily hidden, until disturbed, denied until confronted. Healed if only allowed.

There will be a lot of times in life that you will have to tune out the unbelievers, the naysayers and the dream crushers, because they were sent by the enemy. They were sent to discourage you in hopes that you would abort your mission in life. In hopes that your fear would overpower your faith and you become another statistic. (John 10:10).

Never allow the voice of anyone to silence you or get you off course and leave your destiny behind. Always know that not only can you do all things through Christ who strengthens you, but you were fearfully and wonderfully made. God has the final word on everything and everyone (1 Peter 3:22). Stay strong—you got this!

Be Still and Know That I Am God
(Psalm 46:10 NKJV)

You will face a lot of adversities in life. Some of the turmoil that you will experience will hit you like a mighty earthquake causing what was once sturdy to lose its balance. Shaking the very foundation that you were using for support to weaken to its core. Leaving what is left, unlivable mentally. Emotionally broken, you will look in despair because life as you once knew it is now gone. Only memories that will soon fade away.

During that time of distress, close your eyes and concentrate, not on what things look like, but visualize through faith, the promise that God gave you and begin to put yourself back together, this time allowing your foundation to be built on the word of God. Allow his sixty-six chapters in the Holy Bible to be your rock. Let it guide you toward the life you deserve.

Realize that the things or people that did not survive your earthquake was not meant to survive. They were hindering you from your destination, taking up time in a life that you have borrowed. Your earthquake did not happen by chance. It was a part of God divine plan, a plan to shake loose what was already damaged but not removed, afraid of the pain from detachment. Do not be afraid of what is about to come. "Be still and know that I am God."

If you knew that you could have anything that your heart desire, would you speak it?

If you knew that you could live a life fit only for a king or queen, would you live it?

If you knew that you could be the best at whom you are created to be, would you accept it?

If you knew that you could have a friendship for a lifetime, would you value it?

If you knew that you are on borrowed time, would you appreciate it?

If you knew there is man named Jesus who says you can have that and more ("I am the way, the truth and the life. No one comes to the father except through me" [(John 14:6)]), would you follow him?

Slow Down and Breathe

Because time waits for no man, we tend to be in a hurry and rush through everyday tasks trying to finish before night draws near. We look around us and instead of appreciating what we already have, we allow our wants to tempt us, and we act out of the spirit of the flesh, instead of the spirit of the fruit. We allow greed and jealousy to step in and replace the word and timing of God. We get discouraged in our waiting season, failing to realize that if we obtain something before, we are equipped to hold it, we will only carry it for so long, because through the human eye we see today, we do not prepare for tomorrow or stay focused on the future.

We put ourselves in a race with others, that winning will never be our victory, because it was not our race to run. We hold on to the wrong people and allow those with purpose to walk away. We burn bridges quickly, never knowing if later in life we will ever need to cross again, we allow "we will see when we get there" to justify the actions we have made. Like a game of checkers, we jump over things that we need to get to our destination, not realizing that even though we won, we did not actually win. Do not go through life running and walk out of the will of God

> Be anxious for nothing, but in everything by prayer and supplication, with thanksgiving, let your requests be made known to God, which surpasses all understanding, will guard your hearts and minds through Christ Jesus. (Philippians 4:6–8 NKJV)

Psalm 91:1 (NIV)

Whoever dwells in the shelter of the Most High
will rest in the shadow of the Almighty

You may be experiencing a moment in your life that you feel confused, a moment of being tormented by your mind, visibility only being dimmed because you refuse to look further. A moment that was once full of vibrant dreams now lay dormant, covered by doubt. Life only sustained by being fed false truths based off someone else's failures and never attempted.

You have allowed fear to stand over your shoulders, never speaking, only taking deep sighs. You have allowed negative opinions to hold you bound. Words of previous disappointments are standing at the door of opportunity, but too nervous to walk in. Dreams that you have been carrying around for a lifetime are ready to be birthed, but now you are too scared to push. Words that have been holding you back from allowing your visions to take root, all because it is not being watered in faith. You have allowed yourself to be stuck at a crossroad, because you have been spending your life under the umbrella of someone else. Quit limiting yourself by affirmations of others' opinions and base it off the word of God.

I can do all things through Christ who strengthens me. (Philippians 4:13 NKJV)

Love Despite Of

You have been sitting in anger for a while now, your heart is shattered by someone you loved and trust, you expected them to have your back, because you could only cover what the naked eye could see. Your loyalty to them was pure, when theirs was tainted with betrayal, you considered them a friend, not knowing you were only an associate. Hours have passed by, and your mind is still in a state of unbelief by the actions rendered by those who proclaimed to once loved you. Despite the silent battles that you have fought and the things that you have endured in your time of happiness and in sorrow, you still valued the needs of those that has disappointed you tremendously. Unselfishly you gave when you did not have to give. You showed support during moments that you wished encouragement were returned. Intercessory prayer flowed continuously from your mouth to God's ears, petitioning for a breakthrough all on the behalf of others.

Spectators are now intervening, telling you to get over it, telling you to let go of something, that the pain they do not bear. Scars they will not carry, tears they have not shed, and sleep they will not lose. I have been where you are now, a place where revenge is rushing through your veins, just as strong as flood waters rush through a dam that levee breaks. I know that the hurt you are experiencing is real, you have been knocked off your feet unexpectedly and gasping for air in a place that is polluted. I ask that in your temporary moment of rage that you allow the word of God to permanently comfort you. Instead of being angry, count it all as joy, because God sits high and looks low. In Deuteronomy 32:35, God said vengeance is his and recompense; "Their foot shall slip in due time." Psalm 110:1 says he will use your enemy as your footstool. And in Psalm 23:5, it is said he will prepare a table before you in the presence of your enemy. At this time in your life, continue to trust in God, lean not unto your own understanding, in all ways acknowledge him and he shall direct your path.

John 14:1 (NKJV)

Do not let your hearts be troubled. You believe in
God; believe also in me.

You are probably overwhelmed from beating yourself up by trying to be what and who everyone else in your life needs you to be.
While trying to be who God created you to be. In the process you
feel that there are not enough hours in a day, so you stress yourself
out by trying to fix things throughout the night. Noticing that the
situations are endless because time doesn't stop, nor do problems in
a chaotic world. A lot of times, we take on responsibilities that are
not ours to bear and we become weighed down by trying to carry
them instead of casting them aside or just telling a person "I'm sorry
I can't help you." We feel obligated yet torn because we have taken
on more than we can handle. The sooner that you realize that God
already knows everything that you're going through and how he's
going to bring you out, the better you will be. You are in distress over
problems that are already resolved. Worried over things that rather
you interfere with or not, the outcome is going to always be the same
because God has the final say. Get rooted in your Bible for strength,
because God reminds us through many scriptures to rest in his arms
and do not let your heart be troubled. God is a present help in the
time of trouble. All we got to do is have faith that in due time, our
problems will come to pass. So stop worrying if you're going to make
it, because God has already gone before you and made it.

Dear friend,

I know that you feel overwhelmed as if nobody understands what you're going through. Rest assured God knows that the road you have been traveling has been rough and that you have lost your sense of direction. He sees that your days have become as dark as your nights and your nights appear to be as long as the east is from the west. He understands that you have become weary, and ridden with fear. Your body is asleep, but your mind is still going. Wondering how much longer can you hold on and how much more can one take. Instead of succumbing to defeat, keep walking, refusing to give up or in. Refusing to allow that you will not be anything to hold your back. Refusing to believe that this is how your story ends. Despite your setbacks, continue standing, Standing in expectation. Standing as if what you have been praying for is already here. The First Epistle of Peter 5:12 says, "I have written to you briefly, encouraging you and testifying that this is the true grace of God. Stand fast in it." My friend, I assure you that what you are experiencing is truly part of God's grace for you. The Second Epistle to the Corinthians 12:9 tells us, "My grace is sufficient for you, for my power is made perfect in weakness." So stand as if the day is the day and what you are facing will soon come to pass.

Keep Praying

Even though you might not understand some of the things that you're going through in life or why you're going through it, you must continue to stand and trust in God. Trust in his plans for your life, knowing that in due time your trials will produce a plentiful harvest. During your waiting season things will seem unbearable, you may feel as if you can't take it anymore, but instead of giving up, instead of letting the enemy win, instead of proving to all the ones that said you wouldn't make it, cry out to God and remind him of his promises to you. Remind him that he said whenever you are weak and weary, he will strengthen you. Remind him that he said you can rest in his arms. Ask God to speak peace to your storms. Remind him that he said weeping may endure for a night and joy will come in the morning. Remind him that in Jeremiah 29:12 that he said, "Then you will call on me and come pray to me, and I will listen to you. You will seek me and find me when you seek me with all your heart." Some of your seasons will be hard, and some may not shift for a while. But instead of getting discouraged, continue to seek God, continue to feed your soul and your mind with the word of God. Start a journal and begin writing about your season, your heartaches, your sleepless nights, etc. You might not know it but those same words, will be words that you will be able to help someone else in their season. Keep praying.

Your Calling

You are probably noticing that things that use to bother you don't phase you anymore. Things that people used to say to hurt your feelings, expecting a reaction, you accept it because you realize that all that matters is what God say and how you feel about yourself. Even though you have been continuing to pray for things to change, you have been making it throughout your day growing gracefully. You have been finding joy in your desert and dancing in the rain. Though you want God to do the things that you were in need of, but now you realize that even if he doesn't do it, you are still happy. You are content with the season you're in. You realize that those things that you thought you needed, if push comes to shove, you can do without. Most of all, you realize that when you were in your darkest times, that God was there with you. He didn't leave you nor forsake you, despite all the other prayers he had to answer. You realized that God's love for you was pure and one of kind. While you were in your season you were thinking of all the things you lost instead of paying attention to all the things you were gaining. You realize your worth, you realize that God created you to be more than a go to person or a stepstool for others. You realize that you have a purpose. You have a beautiful gift, and if it wasn't for your trials, your gift would have never been put in use. I know that you're smiling, and you deserve to smile, because you have become the person you were in search of and are on the path, to doing what God called you to do.

Season Shift

I am so grateful that you have made it this far and that I have been able to walk you through some of the things that you were facing. Not only did this book help you, but it helped me also by writing it. I was able to express things on paper that I couldn't share. Writing *Unspoken Words Will Never Be Heard* allowed me to get out thing that was festering in my heart, it allowed me to vent, it allowed me to cry without worrying about who saw or heard me. I was able to be vulnerable, for once I was able to be me. While speaking to you, I was able to speak to myself. *Unspoken Words* helped me to realize my worth. It helped me to strengthen my relationship with God. It helped me to love the person that God created me to be despite my flaws. I spent majority of my life pleasing other people and being there for them, while I neglected myself. I accepted being an option, when I knew that I deserved more and could achieve more if I had faith to pursue. All my life, I was trying to live my life without the person who gave me life, when trying to be there for people I thought I needed in my life. My season was tough, but I wouldn't change my season, because in it I rediscovered God, and I found a beautiful woman who was waiting to live out of that season. I pray that you have become a better woman as well and that you realize your worth. Even though this season has shifted for me, just know it's actually the beginning, to a new me and a new season.

Acknowledgments

I would like to thank God for who he is in my life and for his unconditional love for me. I thank God for directing my footsteps on this journey and for gracefully breaking me, so the beautiful woman that I am today could emerge. I thank everyone who encouraged me with words of support and words of comfort. I thank those who believed in me and for those who didn't know that they were silently inspiring me on my journey. I thank God for my trials, because they are what gave me my greatest testimony and encouraged me to step out on faith and believe in myself and my dreams. I pray that *Unspoken Words Will Never Be Heard* encourages you and motivates you to keep pressing toward the mark. In life, storms will always come, but remember that despite how rough your seas may be or how hard the winds may blow, Jesus is always sleeping in the bottom of the boat. Take care, my friend. God bless.

About the Author

Jennette Smith is an inspiring writer who, like David, is a woman after God's heart. A woman who, despite what she lost during her pruning season, knows that it is God's mercy and his grace that sustained her. She is a woman who realizes that her past does not determine her future, and it is her pain that has paved the way and allowed her to walk gracefully into her calling. Without her adversaries and God's favor, she would not have a testimony to share or the opportunity to turn her dreams into reality. It is what she has been through in life that has pushed her into one of the greatest seasons of her life—a season that she can now tell you from her experience, that you too will make it out of, if you stay focused on the word of God instead of the season that you are in. Jennette prays that through Unspoken Words Will Never Be Heard your faith in God increases as her words encourages you to seek God even more during your trials. It is in your darkness that you will find the most beautiful gifts that will lead you back to the light.

> Let the words of my mouth and the meditation of my heart be acceptable in thy sight, O Lord my strength and my redeemer. (Psalm 19:14 KJV)

Printed in the USA
CPSIA information can be obtained
at www.ICGtesting.com
LVHW091246221123
764614LV00030B/94